FOR ORGANS, PIANOS & ELECTRONIC KEYBOARDS

E-Z PLAY® TODAY

84

ED SHEERAN

T0083994

ISBN 978-1-5400-2228-8

HAL•LEONARD®

7777 W. BLUEMOUND RD. P.O. BOX 13819 MILWAUKEE, WI 53213

In Australia Contact:
Hal Leonard Australia Pty. Ltd.
4 Lentara Court
Cheltenham, Victoria, 3192 Australia
Email: ausadmin@halleonard.com.au

Visit Hal Leonard Online at
www.halleonard.com

The A Team

Registration 4
Rhythm: Folk or Ballad

Words and Music by
Ed Sheeran

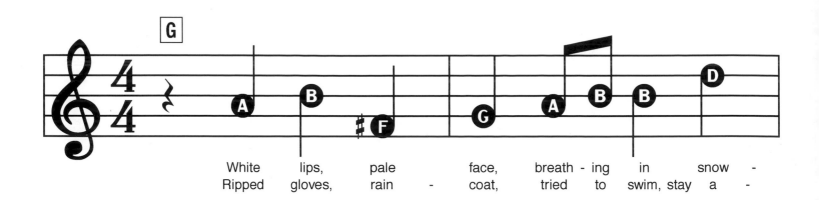

White   lips,   pale   face,   breath - ing   in   snow -
Ripped   gloves,   rain - coat,   tried   to   swim, stay   a -

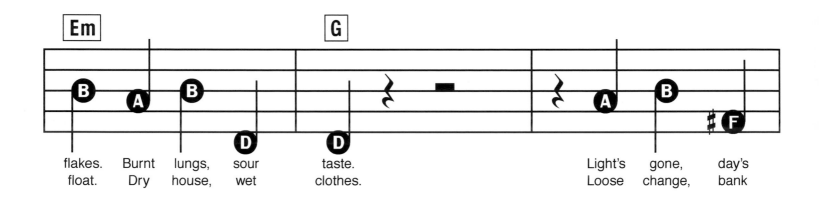

flakes.   Burnt   lungs,   sour   taste.   Light's   gone,   day's
float.   Dry   house,   wet   clothes.   Loose   change,   bank

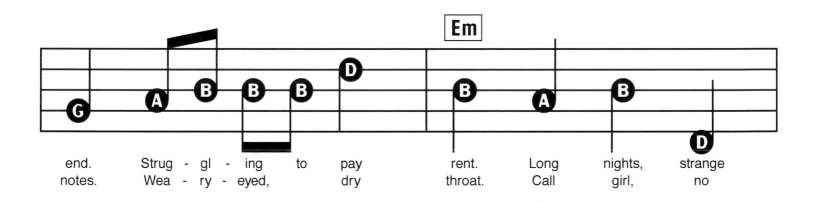

end.   Strug - gl - ing   to   pay   rent.   Long   nights,   strange
notes.   Wea - ry - eyed,   dry   throat.   Call   girl,   no

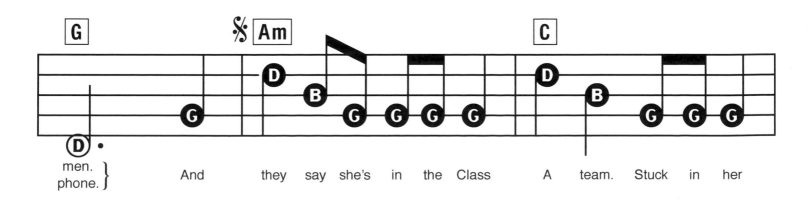

men.
phone.   And   they   say   she's   in   the   Class   A   team. Stuck   in   her

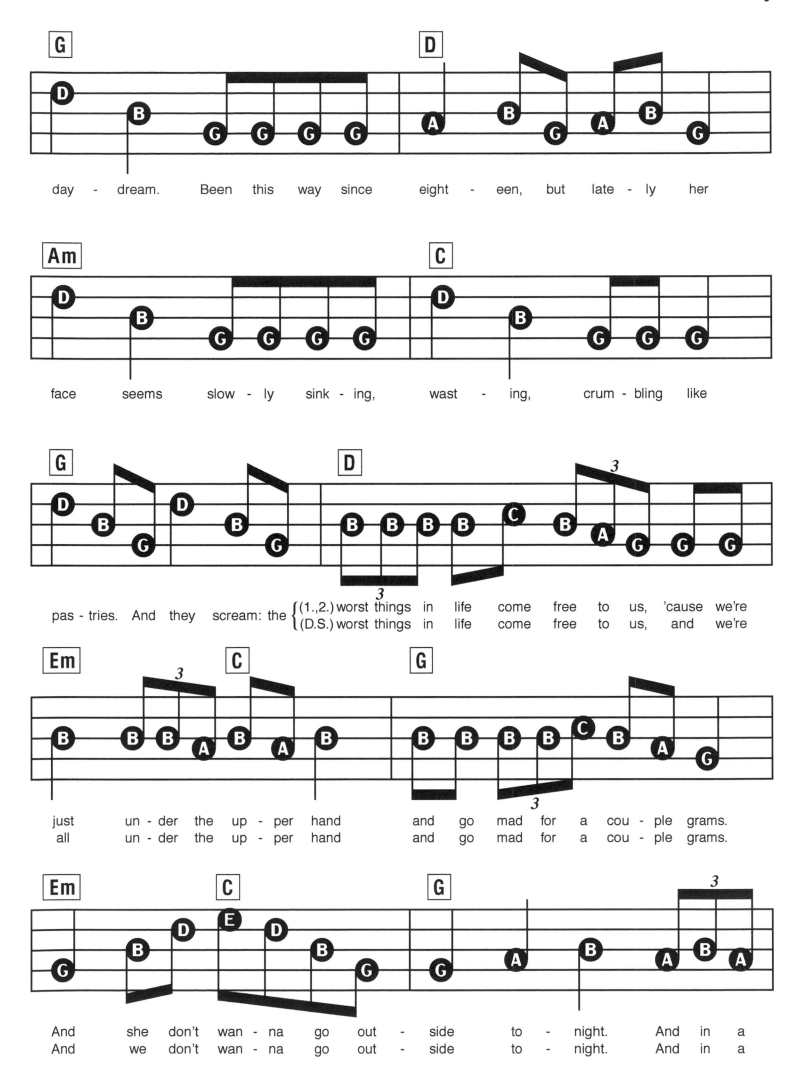

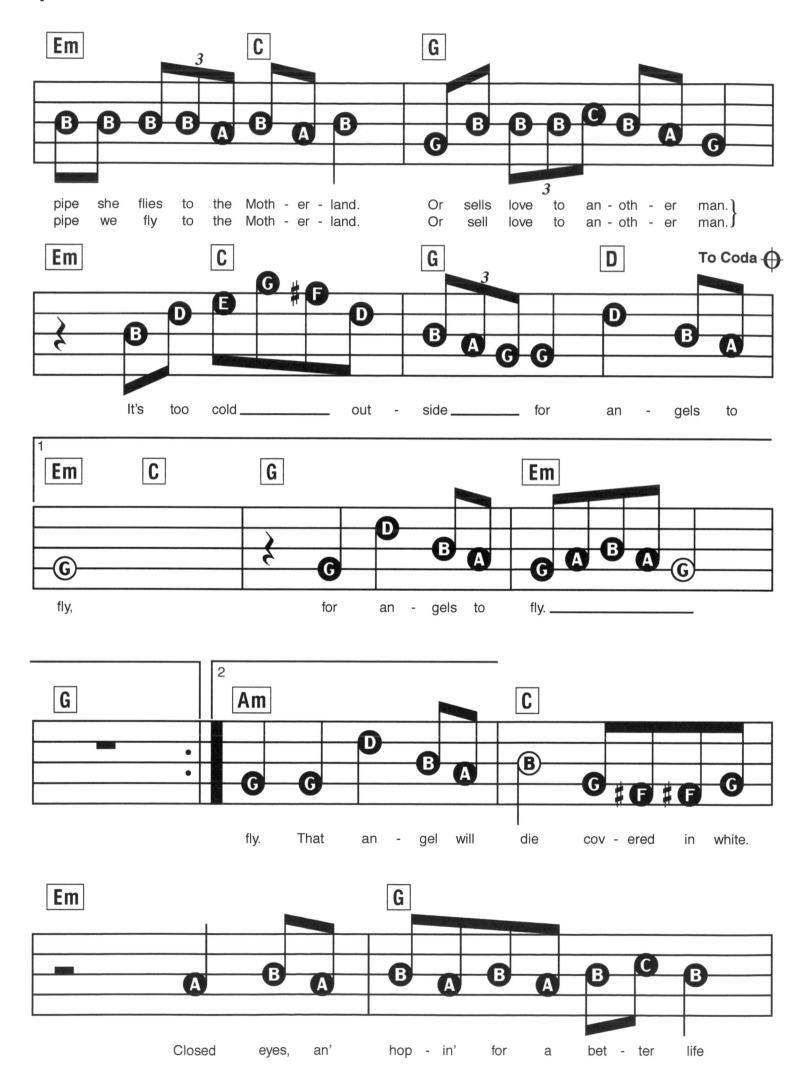

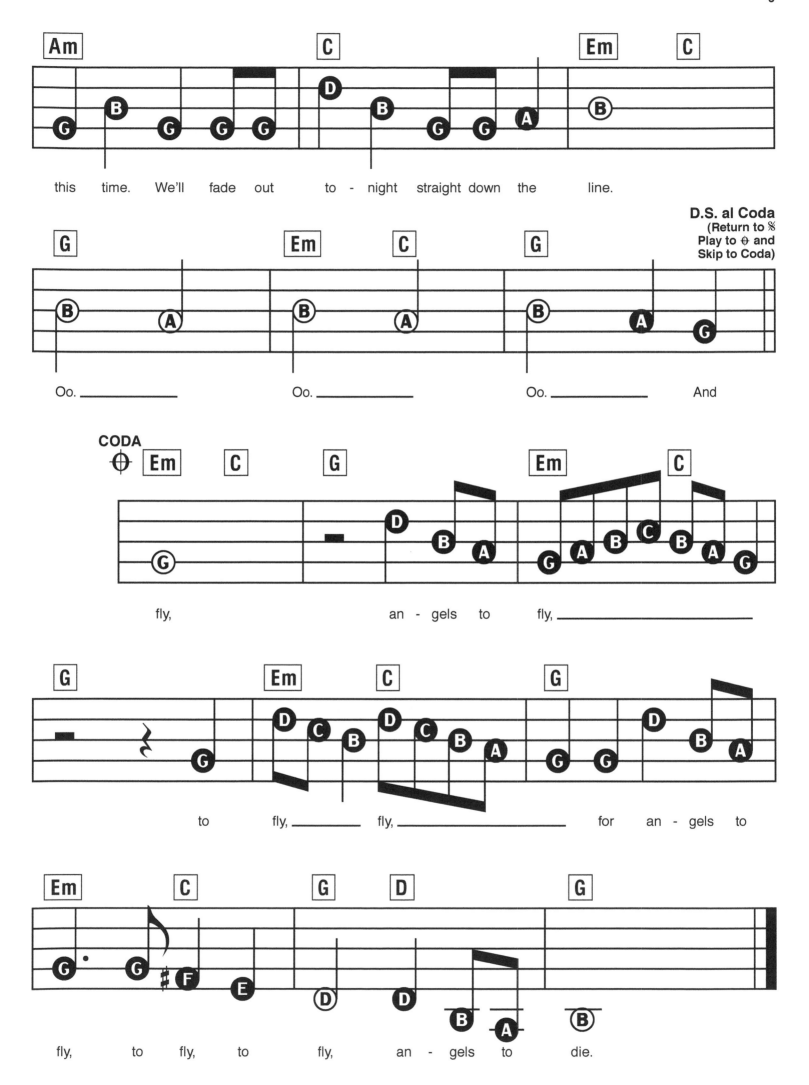

All of the Stars
from the Motion Picture Soundtrack THE FAULT IN OUR STARS

Registration 4
Rhythm: 8-Beat or Rock

Words and Music by Ed Sheeran
and Johnny McDaid

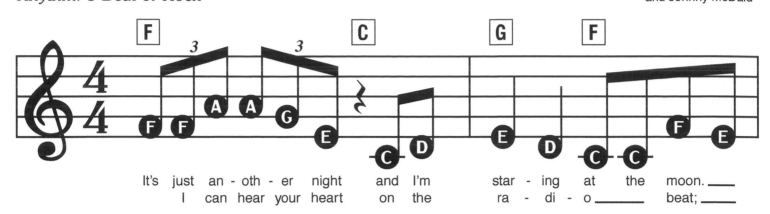

It's just an-oth-er night and I'm star - ing at the moon.____
I can hear your heart on the ra - di - o ____ beat; ____

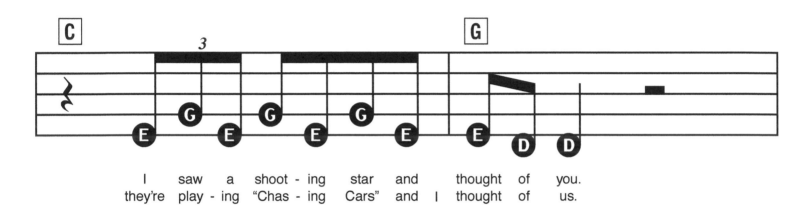

I saw a shoot-ing star and thought of you.
they're play - ing "Chas - ing Cars" and I thought of us.

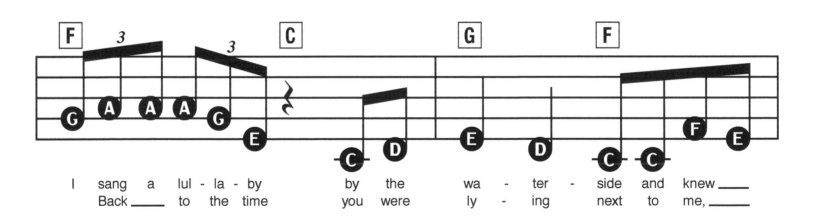

I sang a lul - la - by by the wa - ter - side and knew ____
Back ____ to the time you were ly - ing next to me, ____

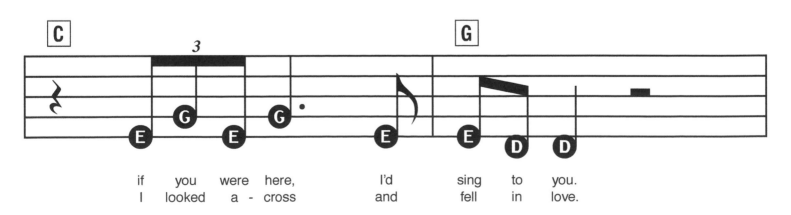

if you were here, I'd sing to you.
I looked a - cross and fell in love.

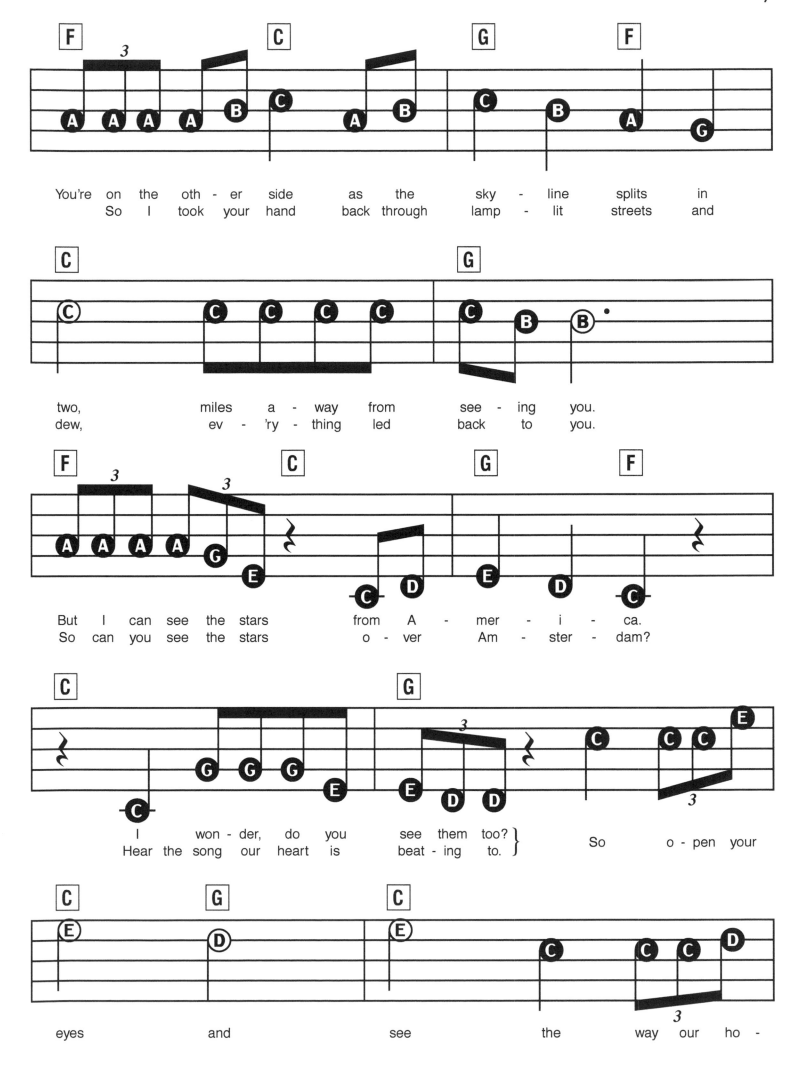

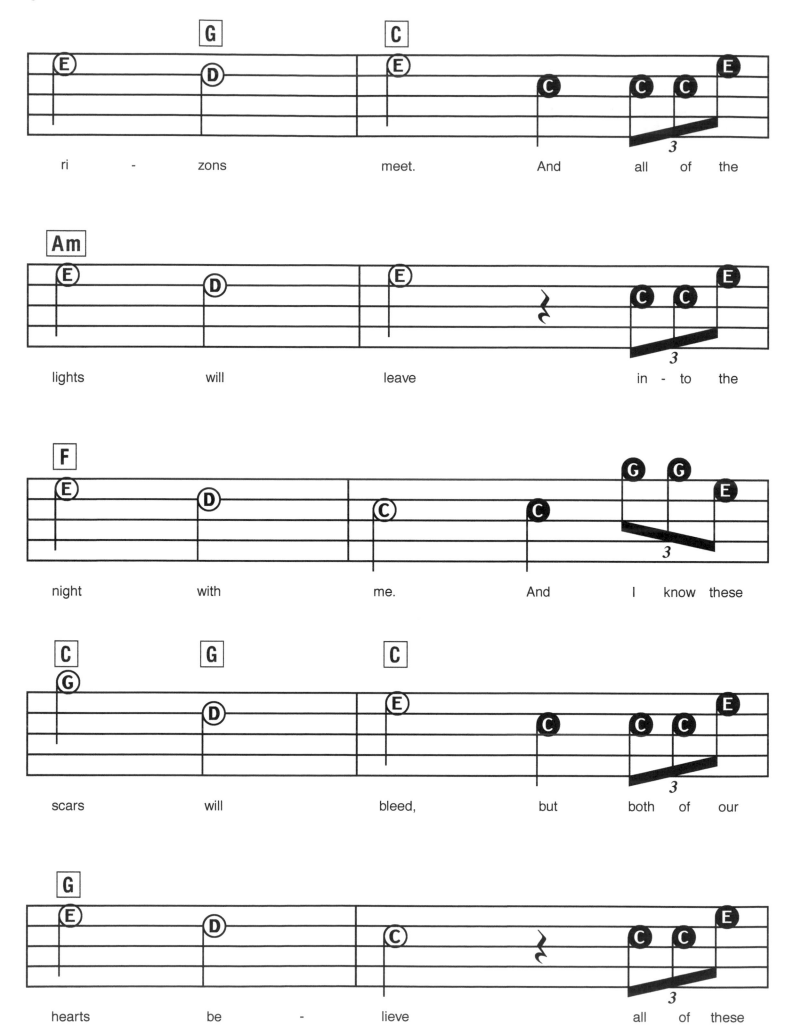

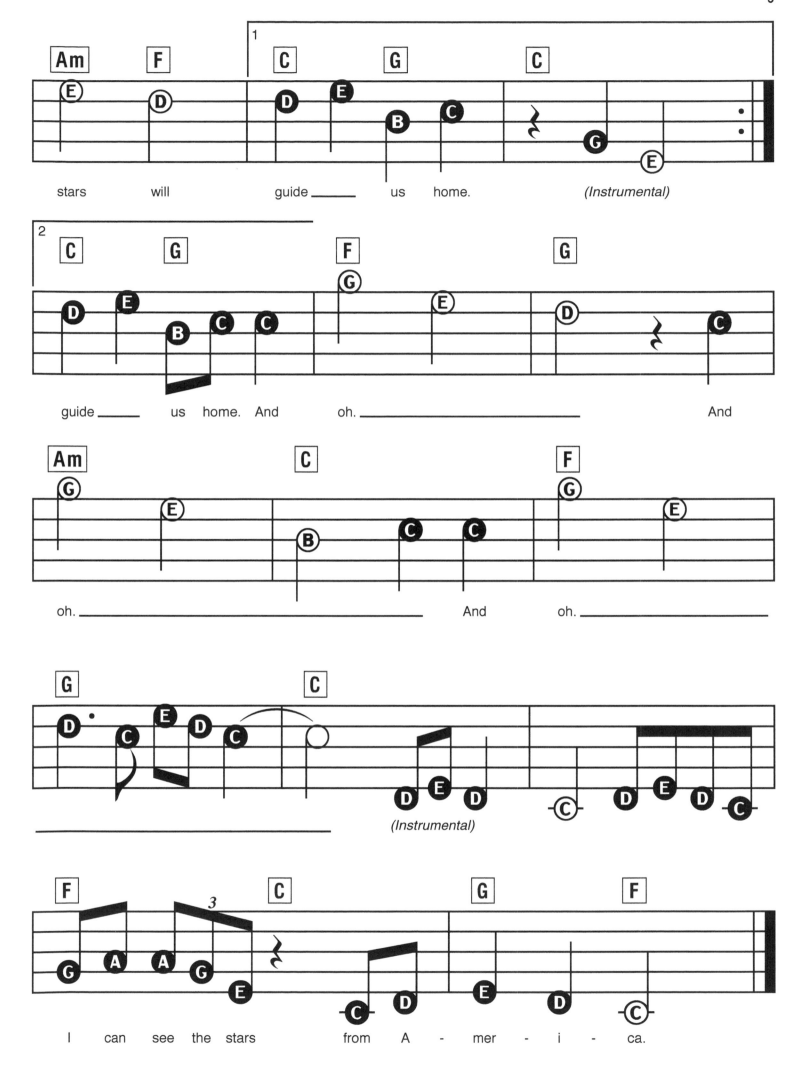

Castle on the Hill

Registration 4
Rhythm: Dance or Rock

Words and Music by Ed Sheeran
and Benjamin Levin

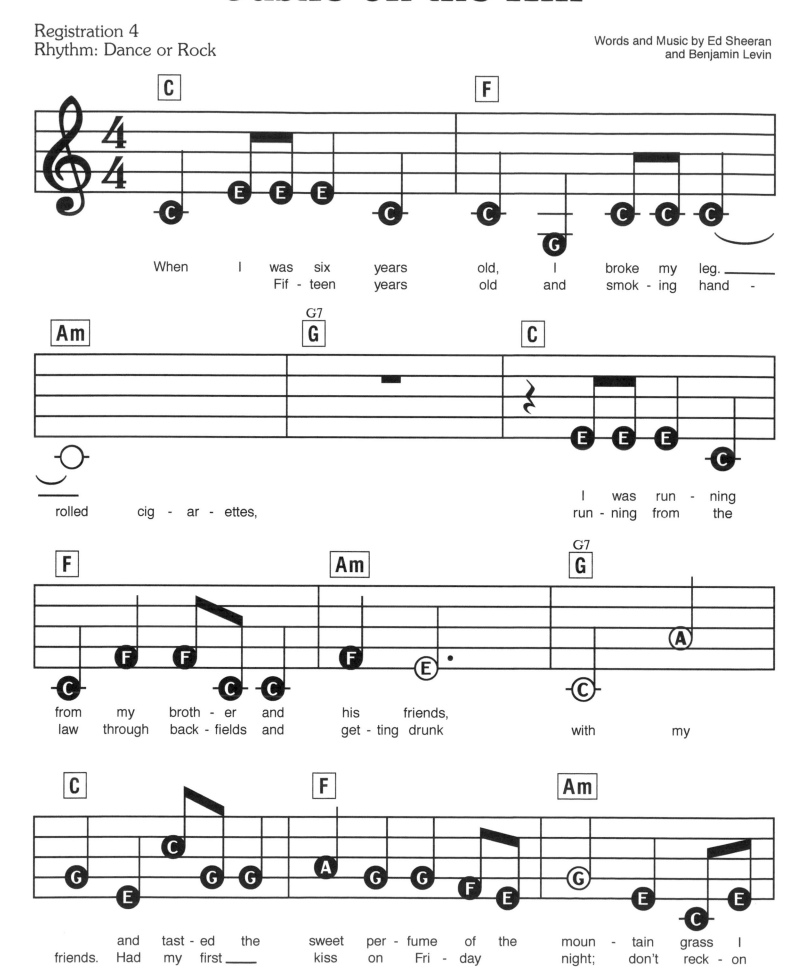

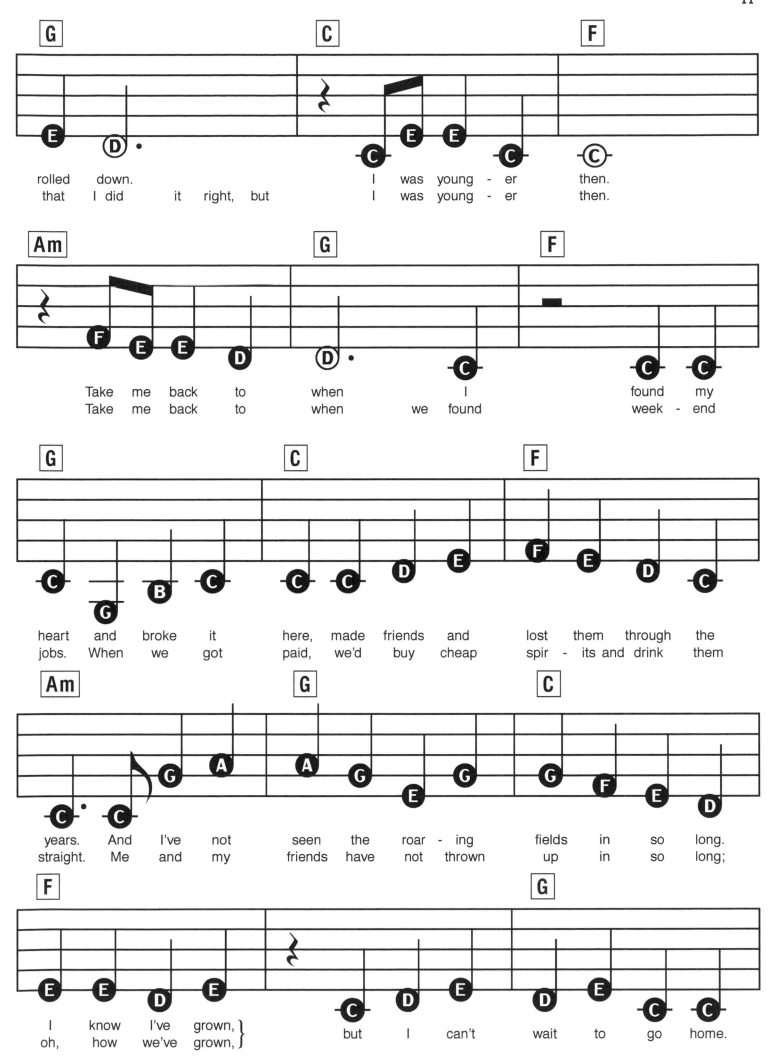

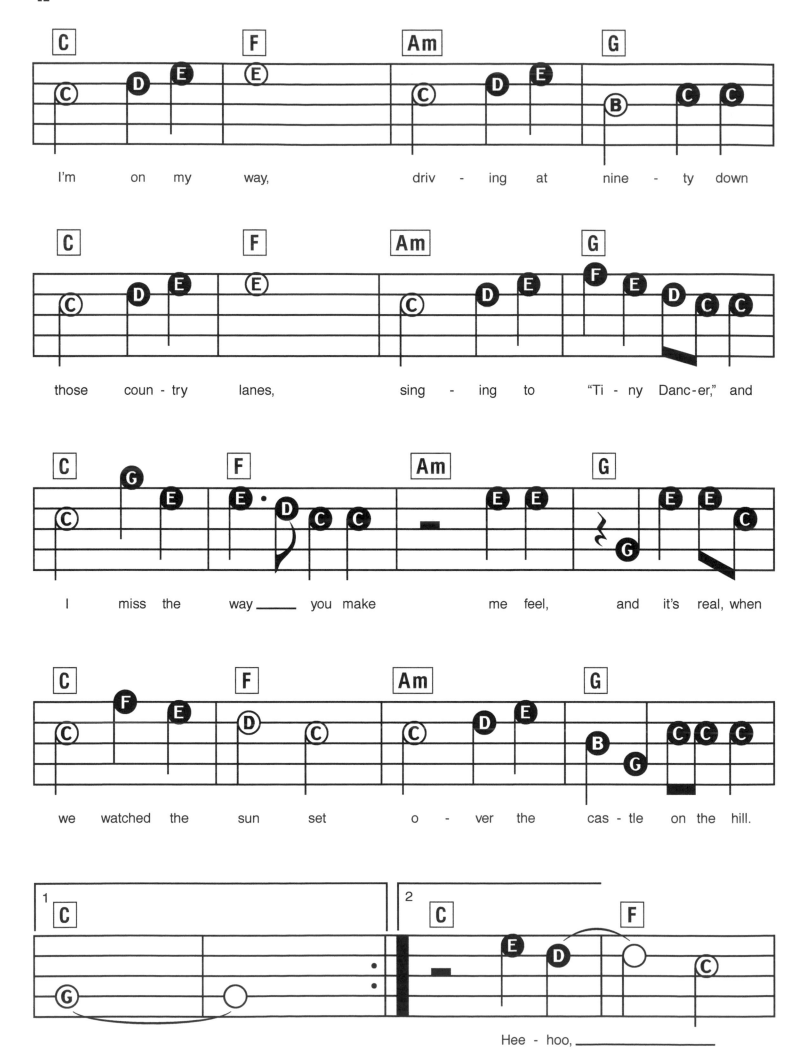

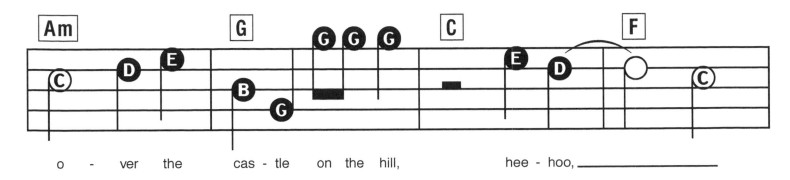

o - ver the cas - tle on the hill, hee - hoo, _____

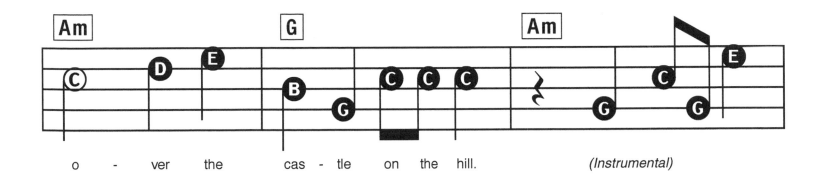

o - ver the cas - tle on the hill. *(Instrumental)*

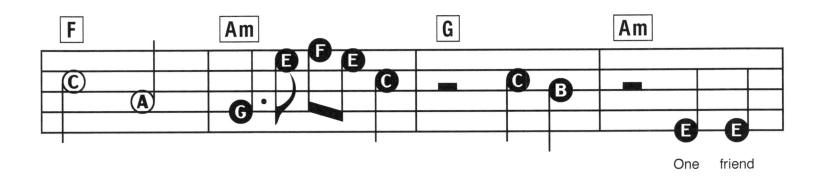

One friend

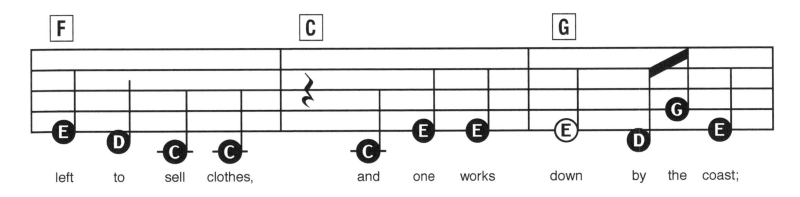

left to sell clothes, and one works down by the coast;

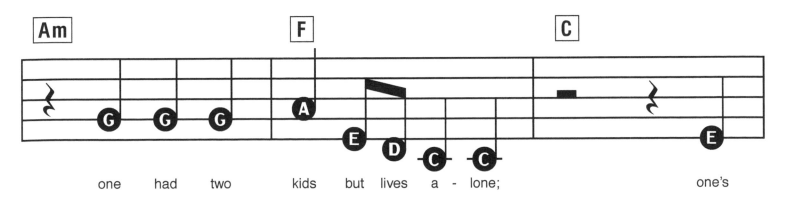

one had two kids but lives a - lone; one's

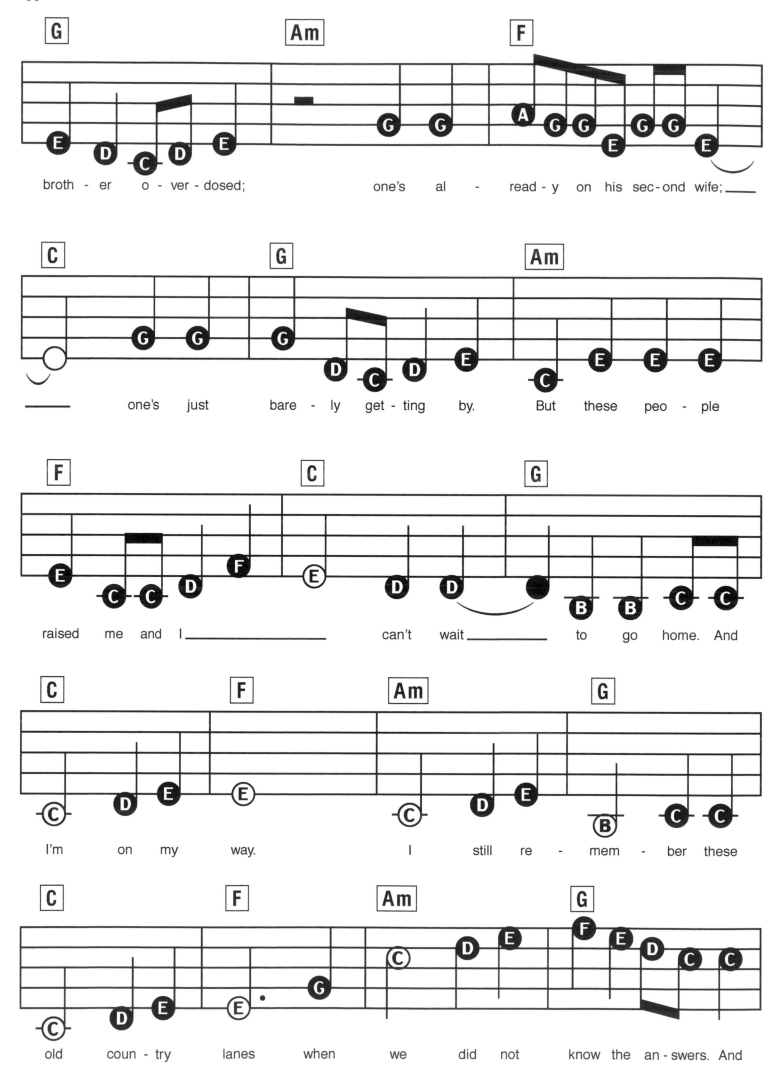

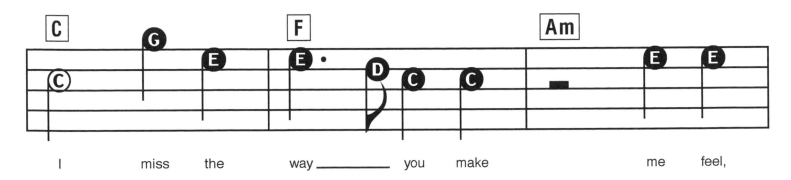

I miss the way _____ you make me feel,

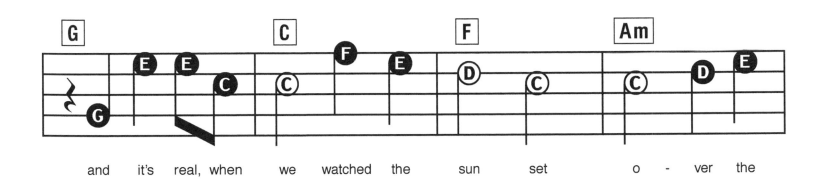

and it's real, when we watched the sun set o - ver the

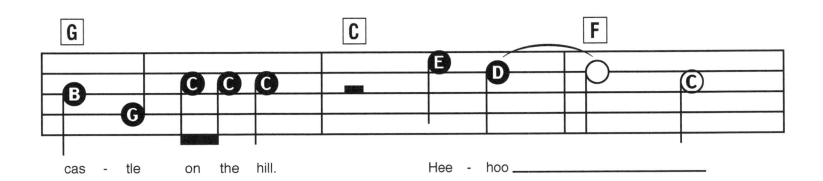

cas - tle on the hill. Hee - hoo _____

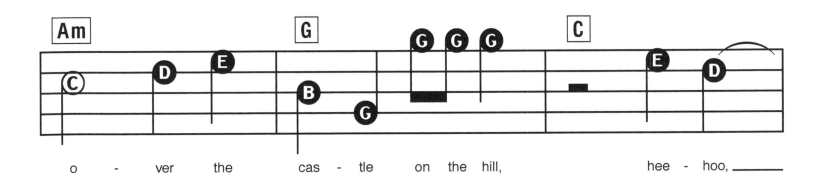

o - ver the cas - tle on the hill, hee - hoo, _____

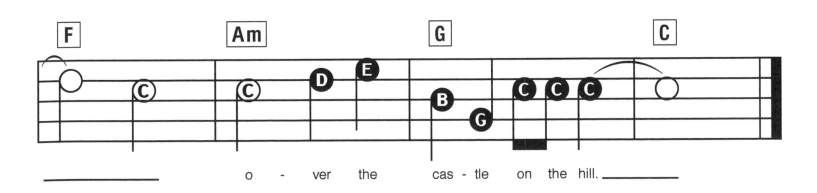

_____ o - ver the cas - tle on the hill. _____

Don't

Registration 8
Rhythm: Funk or Rock

Words and Music by Ed Sheeran,
Dawn Robinson, Benjamin Levin, Raphael Saadiq,
Ali Jones-Muhammad and Conesha Owens

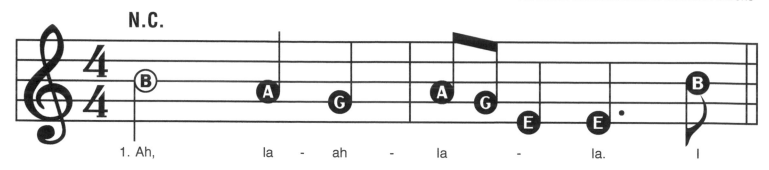

1. Ah, la - ah - la - la. I

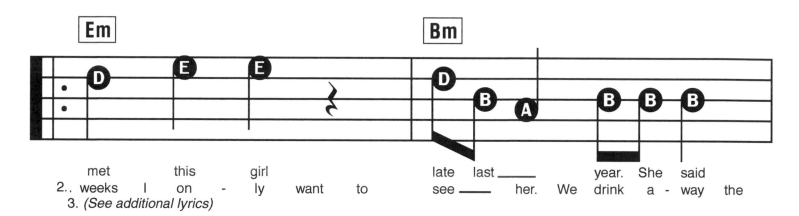

met this girl late last _____ year. She said
2. .. weeks I on - ly want to see _____ her. We drink a - way the
3. (See additional lyrics)

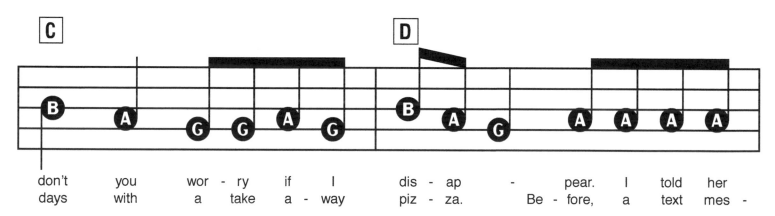

don't you wor - ry if I dis - ap - pear. I told her
days with a take a - way piz - za. Be - fore, a told text mes -

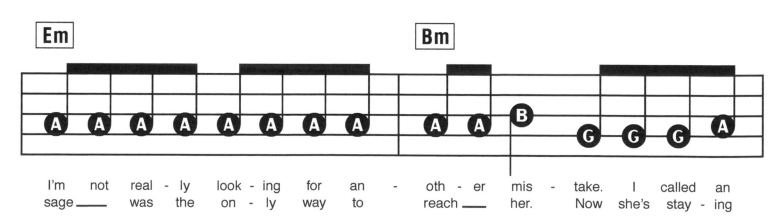

I'm not real - ly look - ing for an - oth - er mis - take. I called an
sage _____ was the on - ly way to reach _____ her. Now she's stay - ing

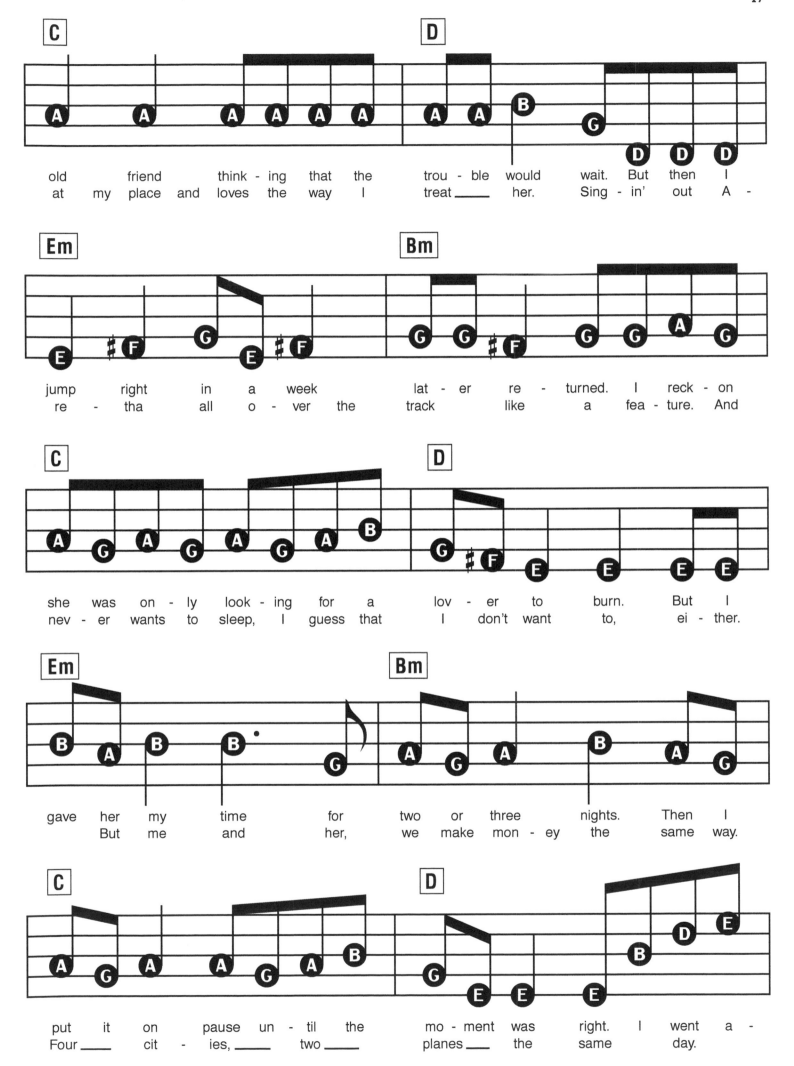

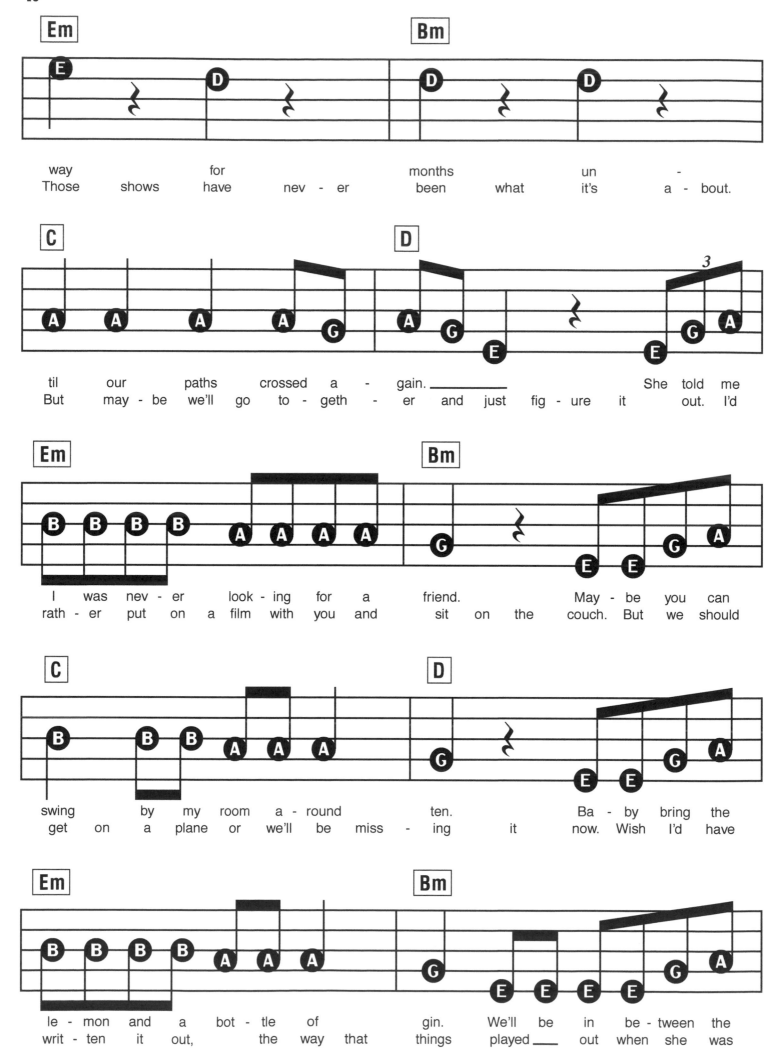

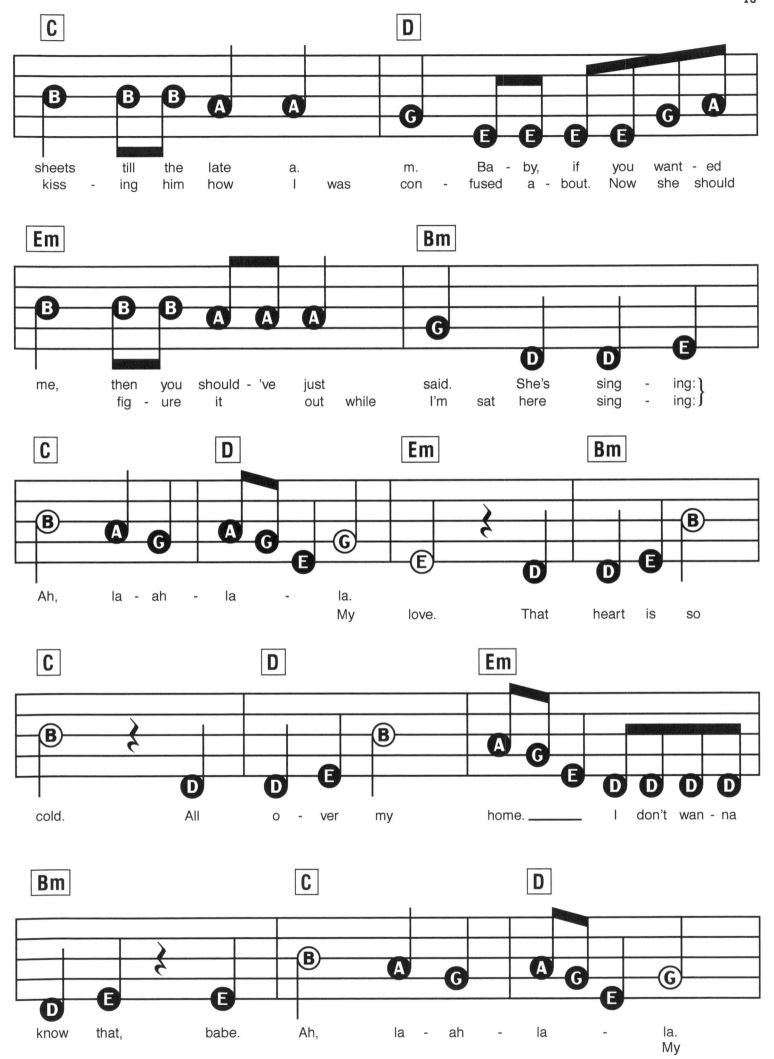

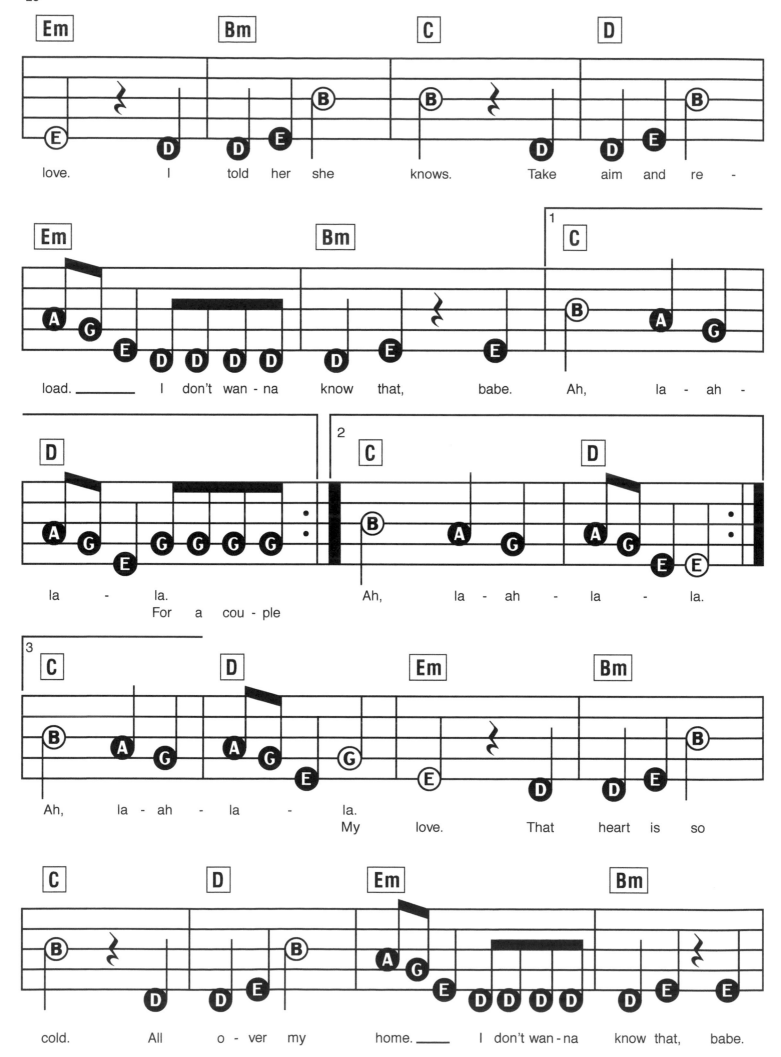

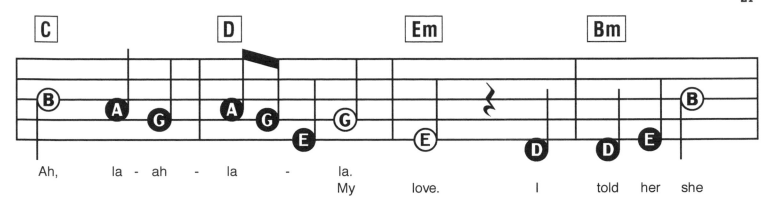

Ah, la - ah - la - la.
My love. I told her she

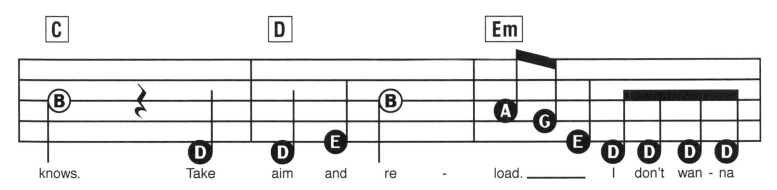

knows. Take aim and re - load. _____ I don't wan - na

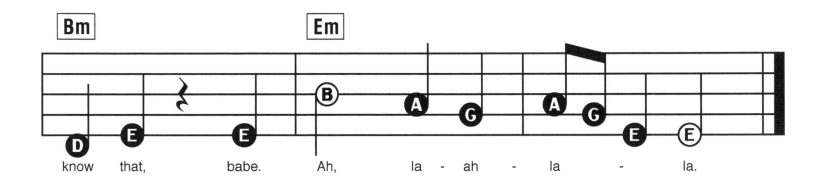

know that, babe. Ah, la - ah - la - la.

Additional Lyrics

3. [Knock, knock, knock] on my hotel door.
   I don't even know if she knows what for.
   She was crying on my shoulder.
   I already told ya.
   Trust and respect is what we do this for.
   I never intended to be next.
   But you didn't need to take him to bed, that's all.
   And I never saw him as a threat.
   Until you disappeared with him to have sex, of course.
   It's not like we were both on tour.
   We were staying on the same hotel floor.
   And I wasn't looking for a promise or commitment,
   But it was never just fun and I thought you were different.
   This is not the way you realize what you wanted.
   It's a bit too much too late, if I'm honest.
   All this time, God knows, I'm singin':

Give Me Love

Registration 4
Rhythm: Slow Rock or 6/8 March

Words and Music by Ed Sheeran,
Chris Leonard and Jake Gosling

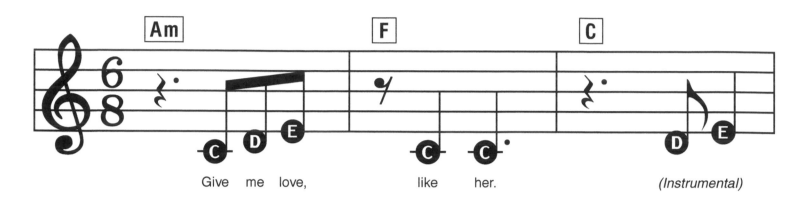

Give me love, like her. (Instrumental)

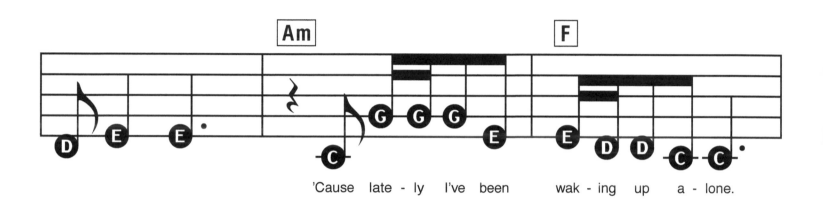

'Cause late-ly I've been wak-ing up a-lone.

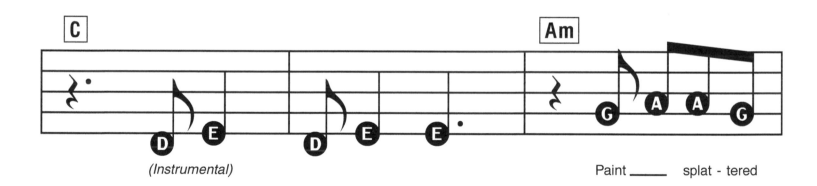

(Instrumental) Paint _____ splat-tered

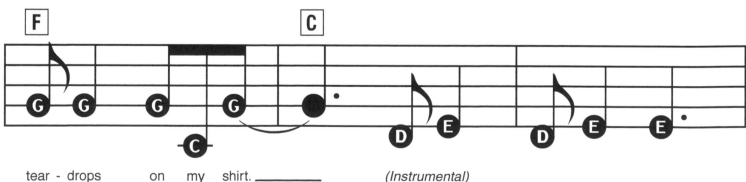

tear-drops on my shirt. _____ (Instrumental)

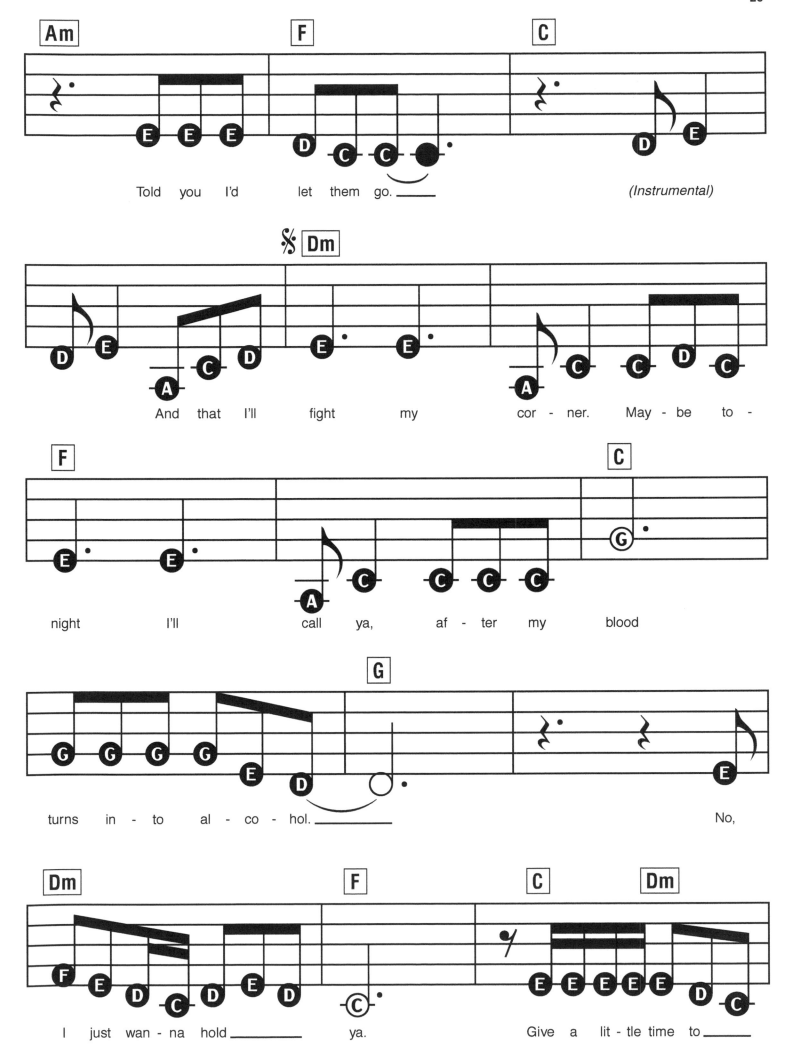

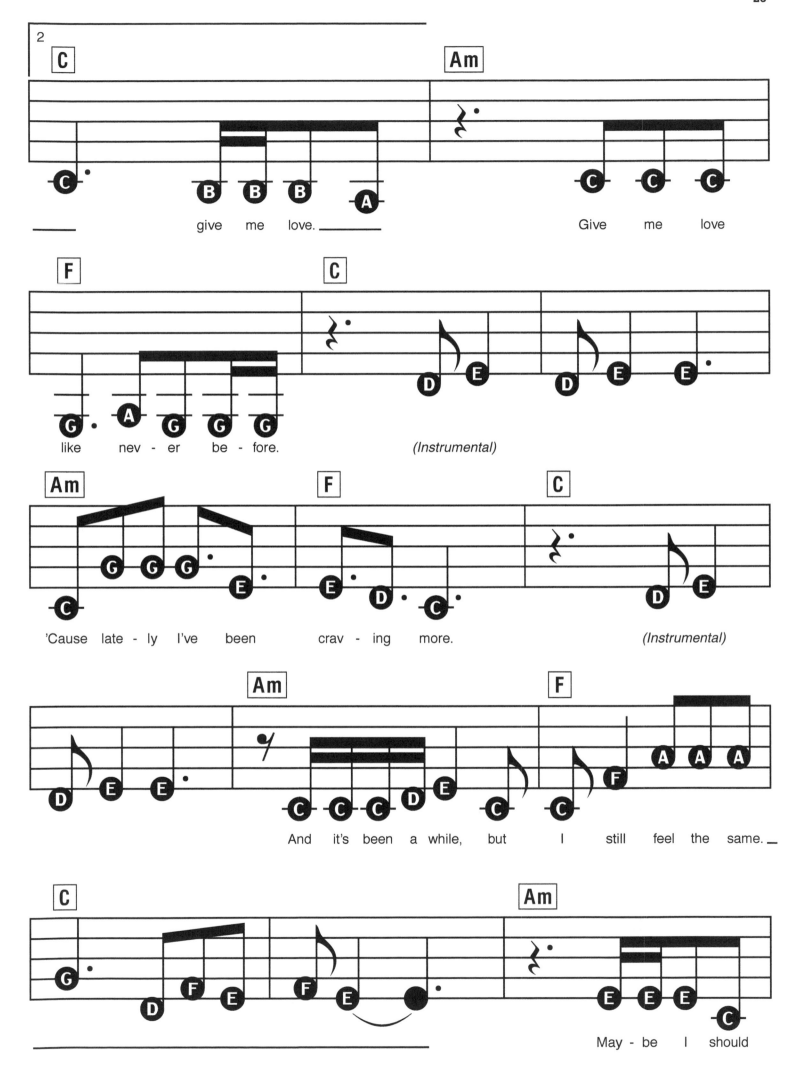

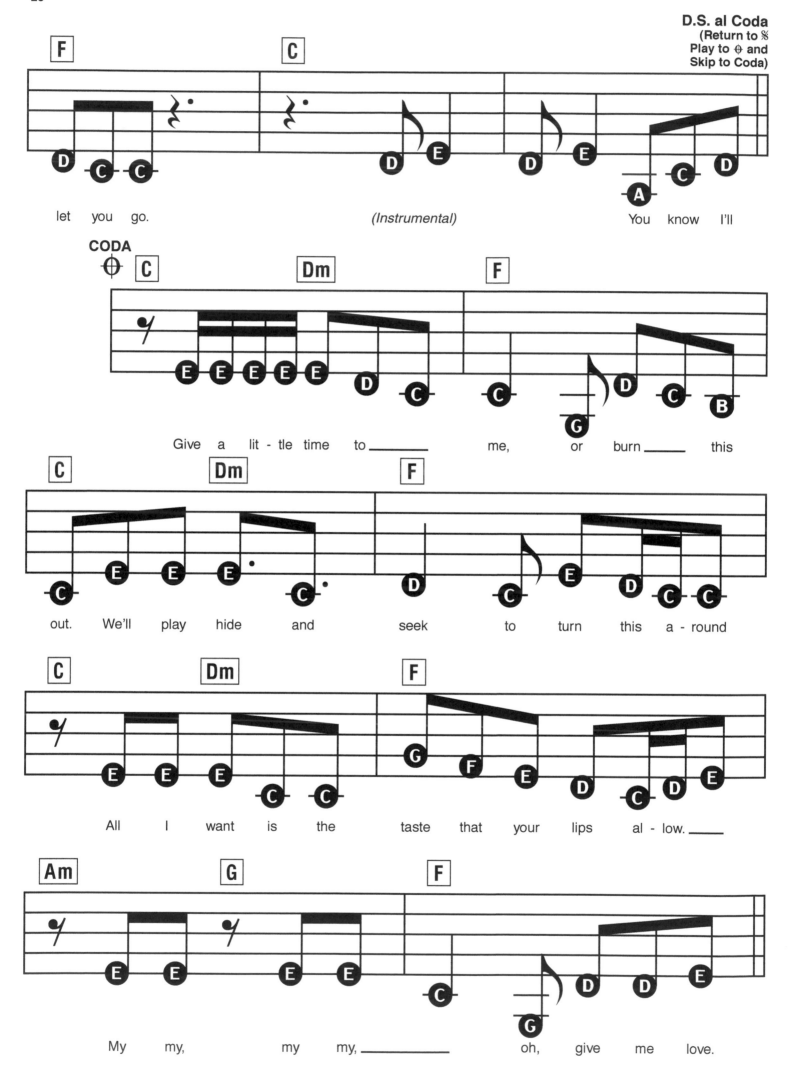

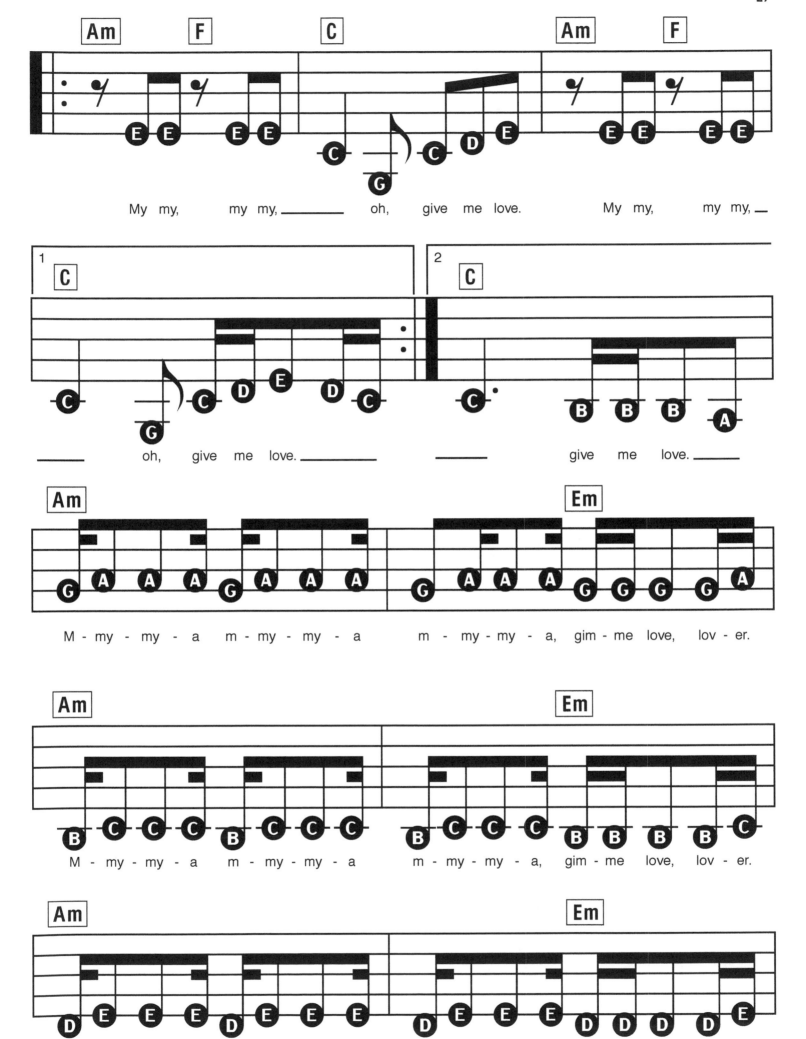

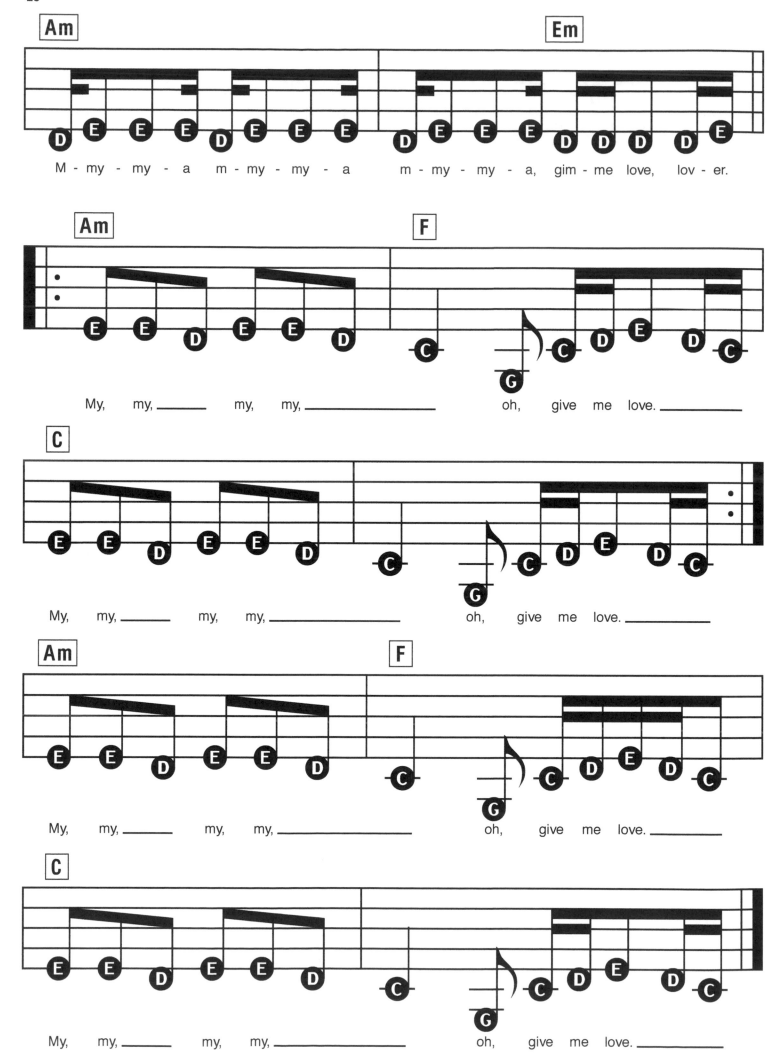

How Would You Feel
(Paean)

Registration 8
Rhythm: 4/4 Ballad

Words and Music by
Ed Sheeran

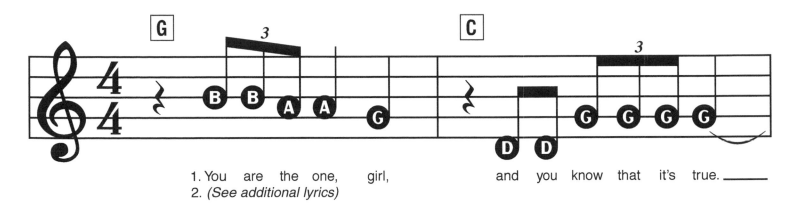

1. You are the one, girl, and you know that it's true.
2. (See additional lyrics)

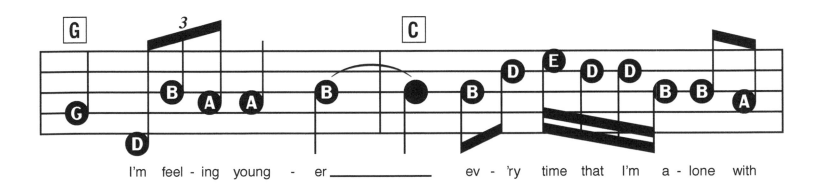

(Instrumental)

I'm feel - ing young - er _____ ev - 'ry time that I'm a - lone with

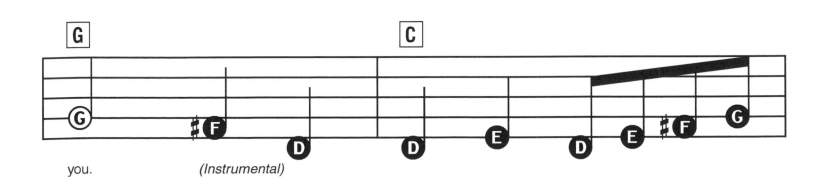

you. (Instrumental)

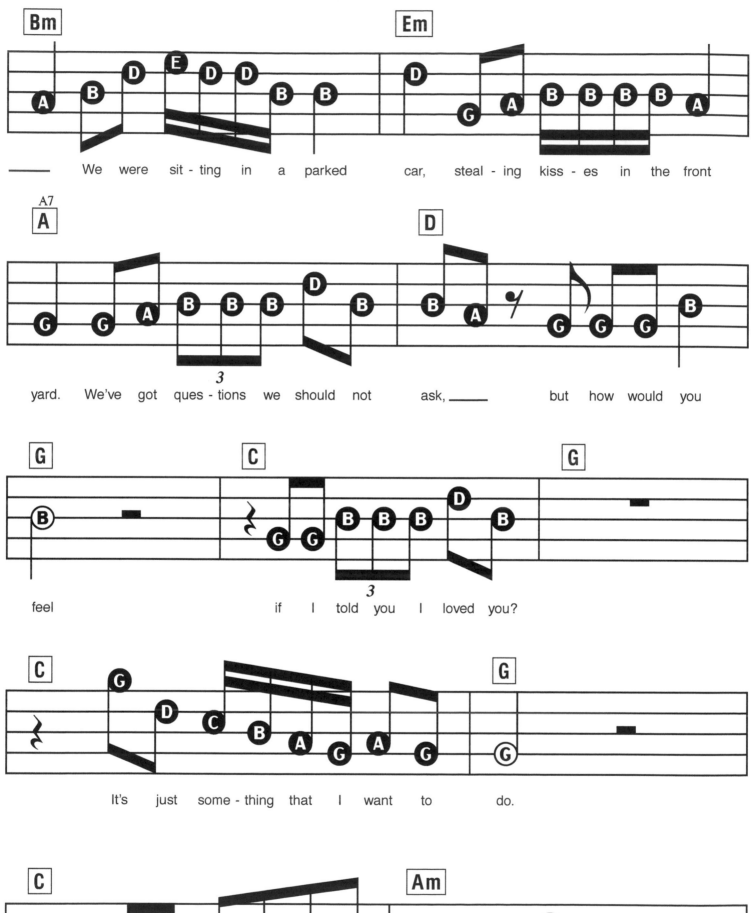

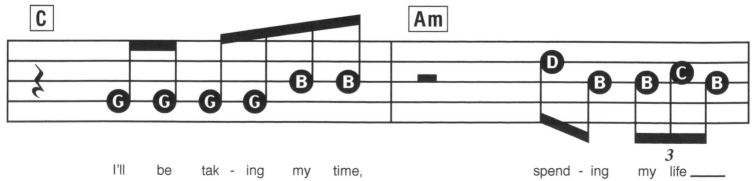

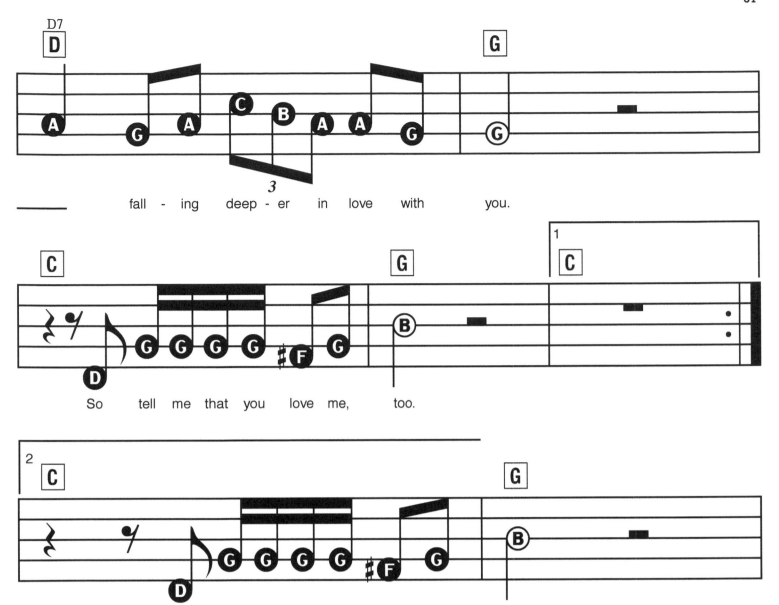

fall - ing deep - er in love with you.

So tell me that you love me, too.

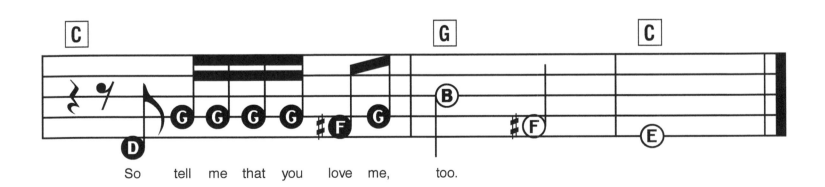

So tell me that you love me, too.

So tell me that you love me, too.

Additional Lyrics

2. In the summer as the lilacs bloom
Love flows deeper than a river
Ev'ry moment I spend with you.
We were sat upon our best friend's roof,
I had both of my arms 'round you
Watching the sunrise replace the moon.
How would you feel
If I told you I loved you?

I See Fire

Registration 4
Rhythm: 4/4 Ballad or Folk

Words and Music by
Ed Sheeran

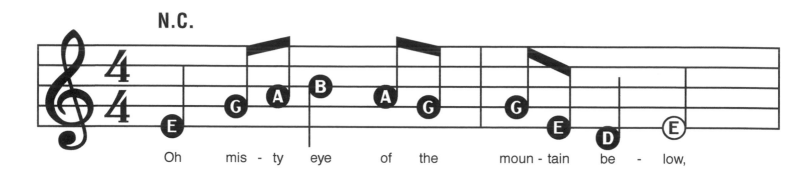

Oh mis - ty eye of the moun - tain be - low,

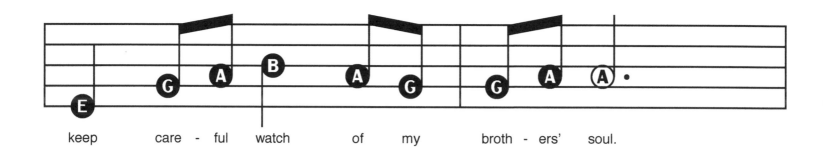

keep care - ful watch of my broth - ers' soul.

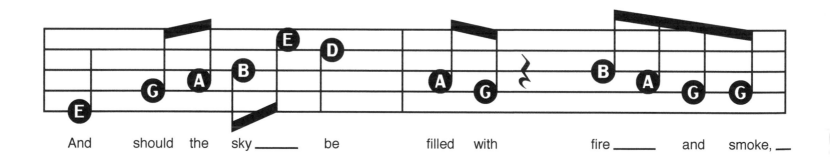

And should the sky ____ be filled with fire ____ and smoke, __

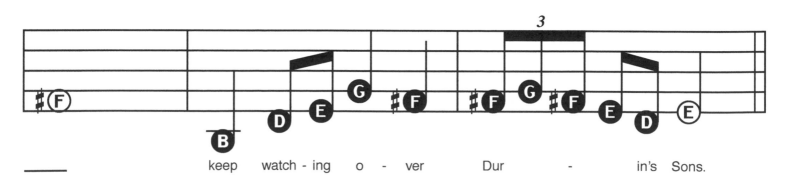

____ keep watch - ing o - ver Dur - in's Sons.

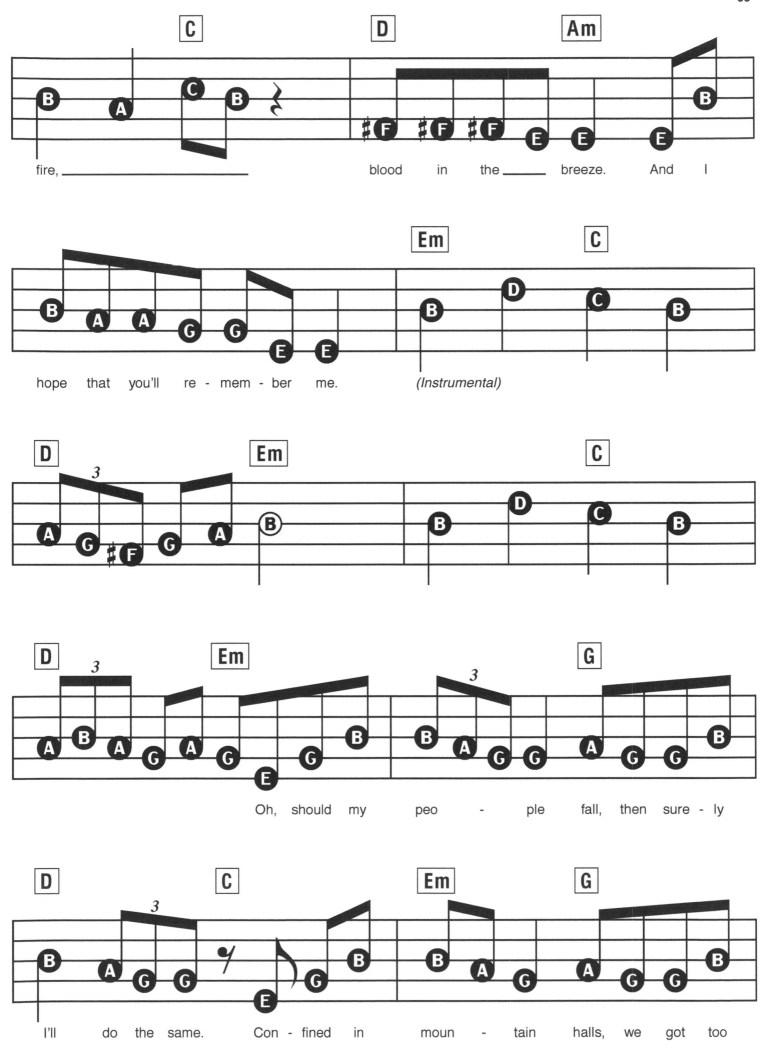

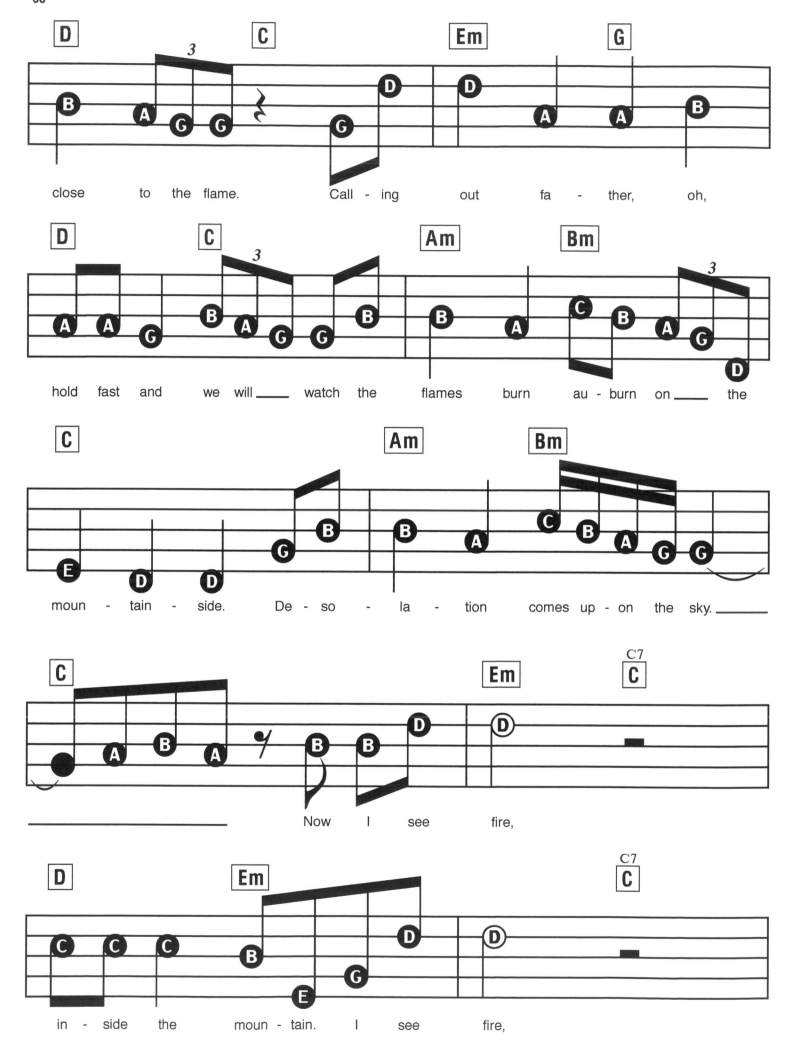

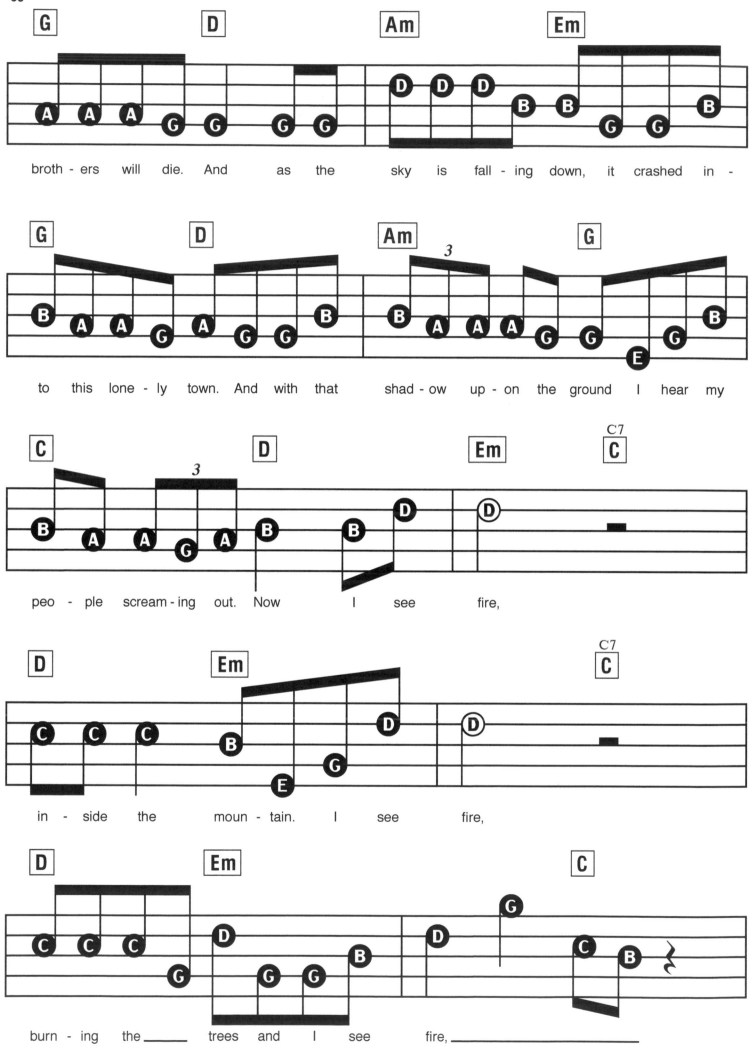

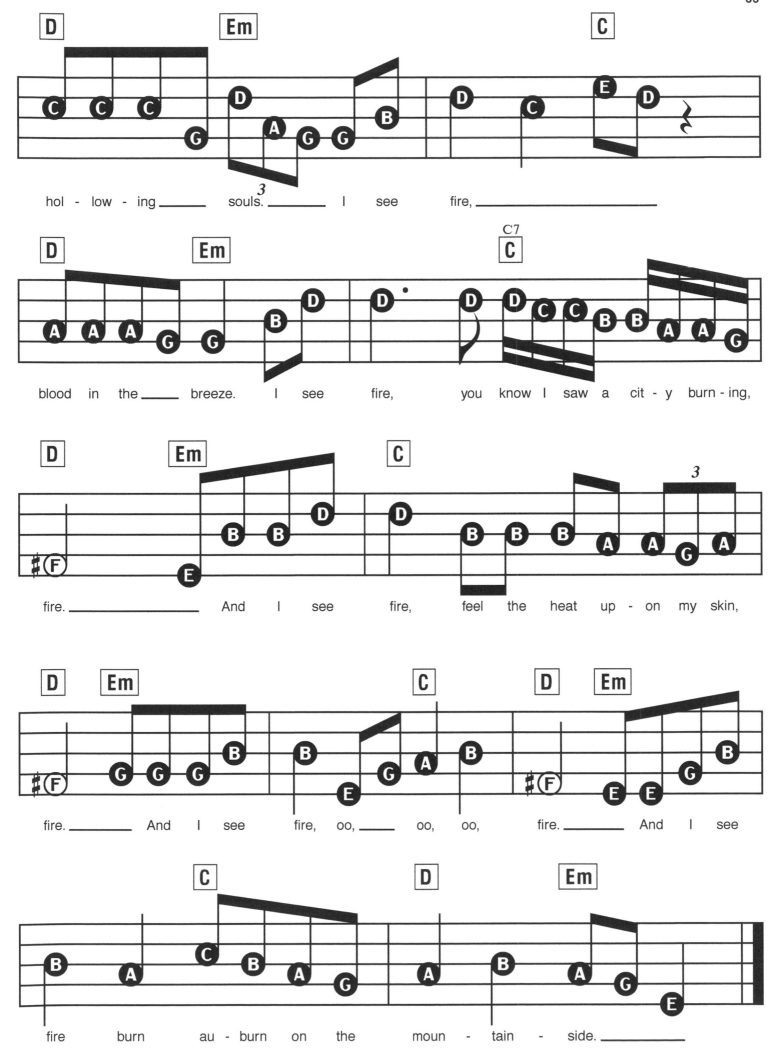

Kiss Me

Registration 4
Rhythm: 4/4 Ballad or Folk

Words and Music by Ed Sheeran,
Julie Frost, Justin Franks and Ernest Wilson

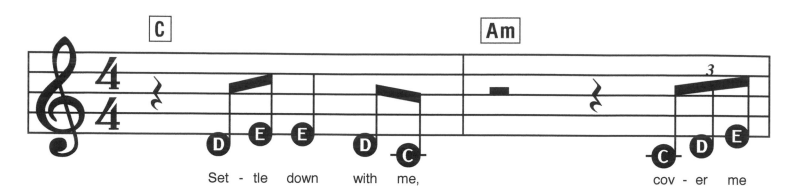

Set - tle down with me, cov - er me

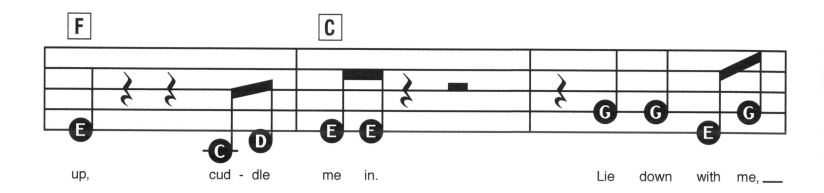

up, cud - dle me in. Lie down with me, ___

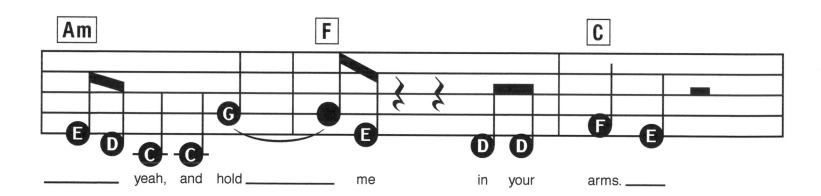

___ yeah, and hold ___ me in your arms. ___

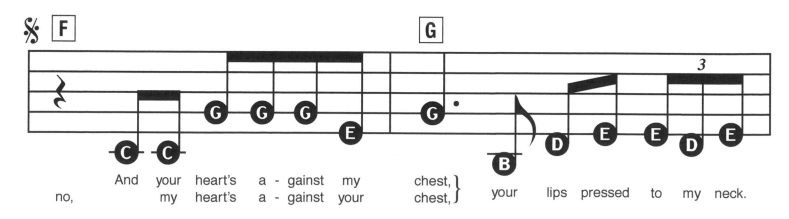

And your heart's a - gainst my chest,
no, my heart's a - gainst your chest, your lips pressed to my neck.

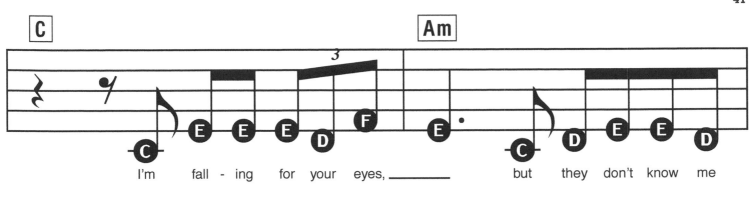

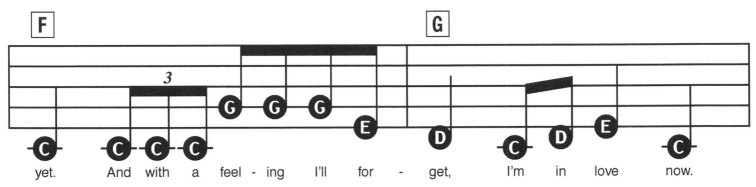

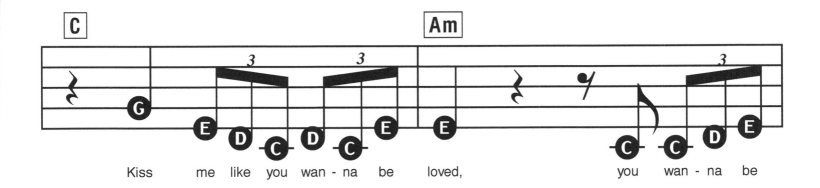

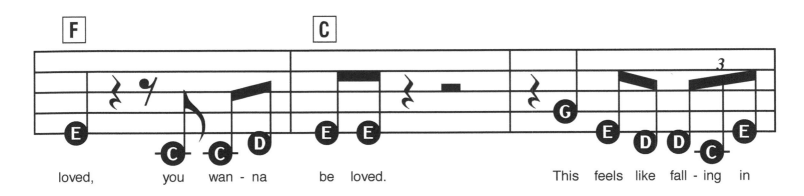

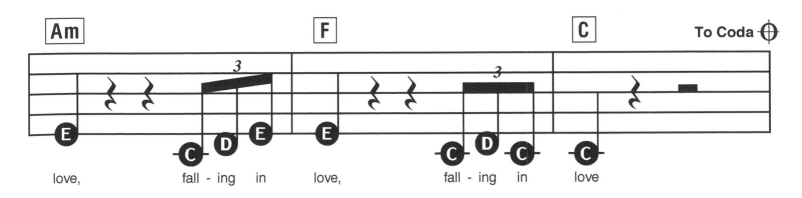

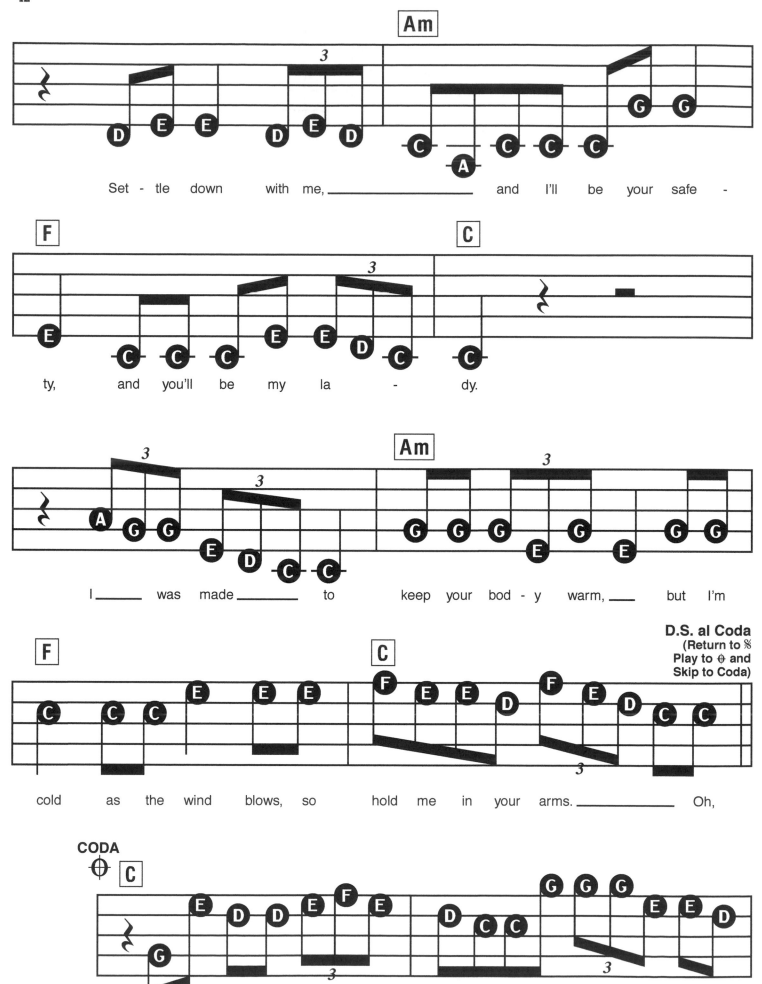

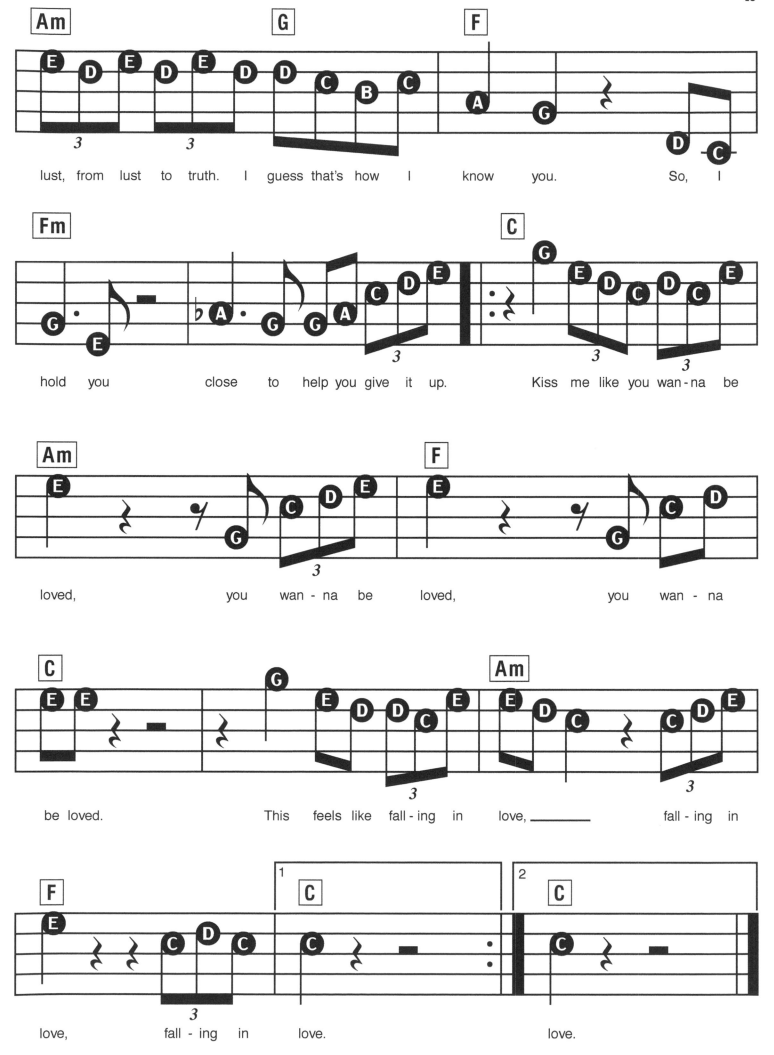

Lego House

Registration 4
Rhythm: Folk or Rock

Words and Music by Ed Sheeran,
Chris Leonard and Jake Gosling

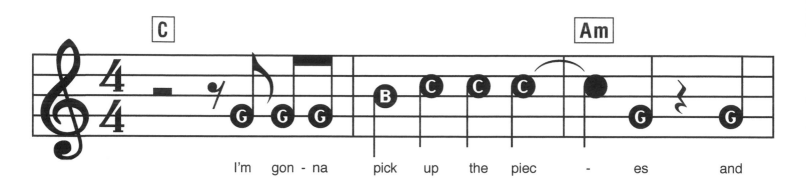

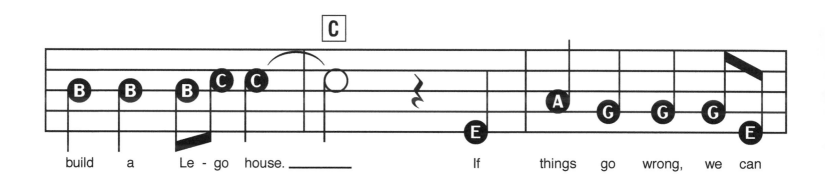

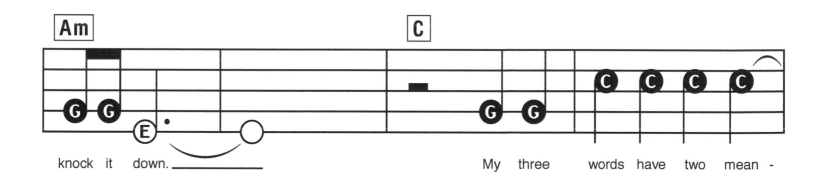

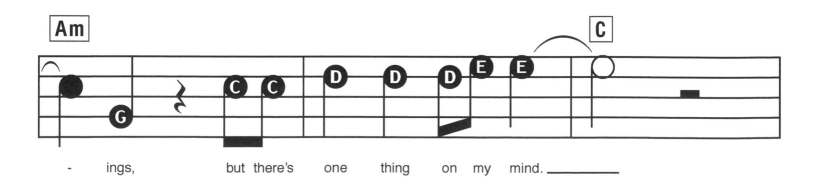

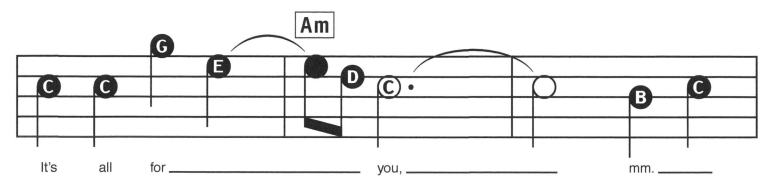

It's all for _____ you, _____ mm. _____

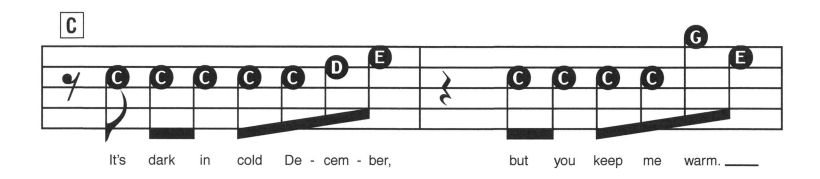

It's dark in cold De - cem - ber, but you keep me warm. ____

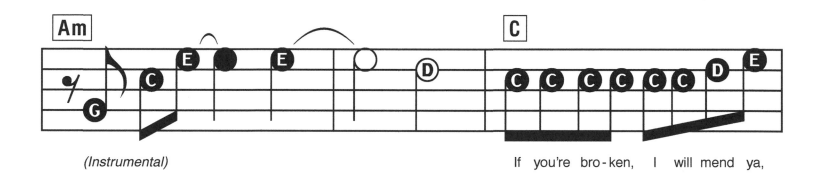

(Instrumental) If you're bro - ken, I will mend ya,

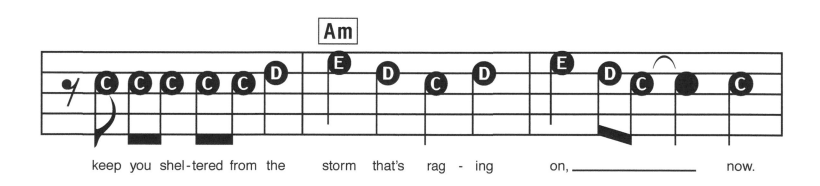

keep you shel - tered from the storm that's rag - ing on, _____ now.

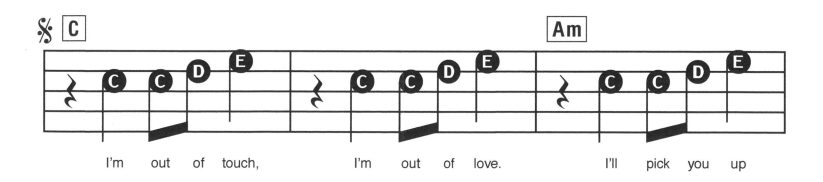

I'm out of touch, I'm out of love. I'll pick you up

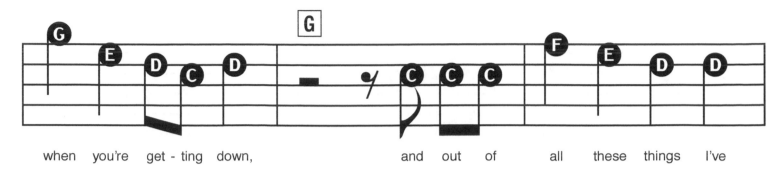

when you're get-ting down, and out of all these things I've

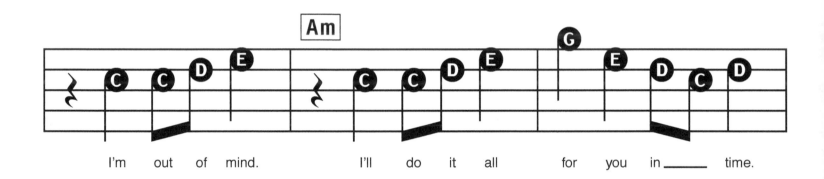

done, I think I love you bet-ter now. I'm out of sight,

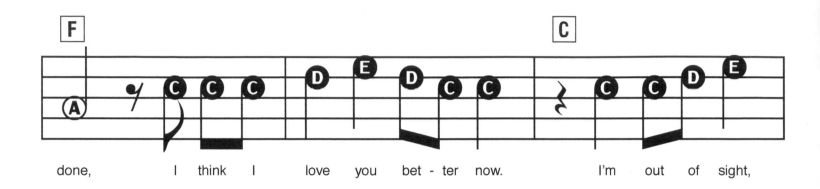

I'm out of mind. I'll do it all for you in ____ time.

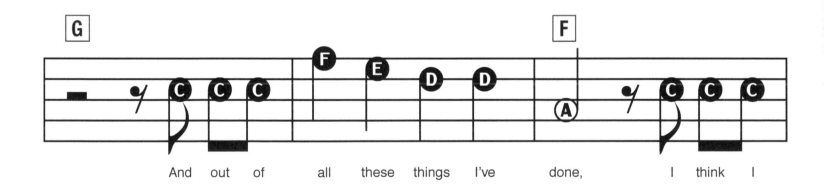

And out of all these things I've done, I think I

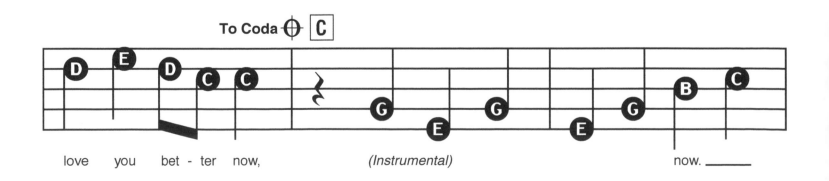

love you bet-ter now, (Instrumental) now. ____

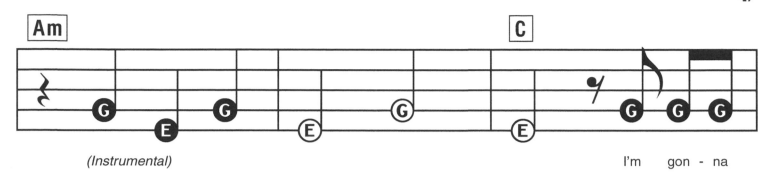

(Instrumental) I'm gon - na

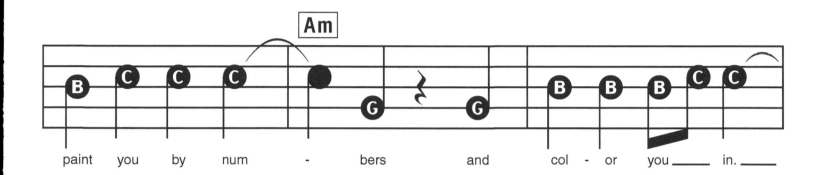

paint you by num - bers and col - or you ___ in. ___

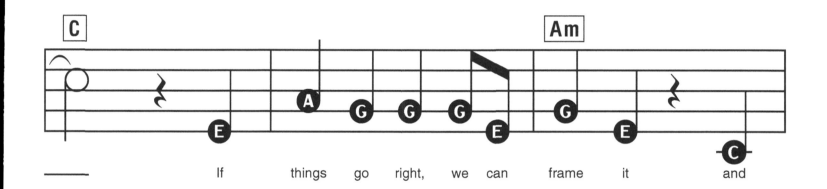

___ If things go right, we can frame it and

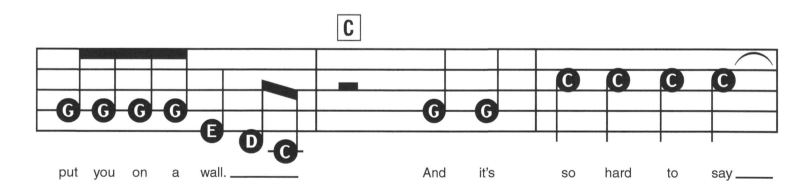

put you on a wall. ___ And it's so hard to say ___

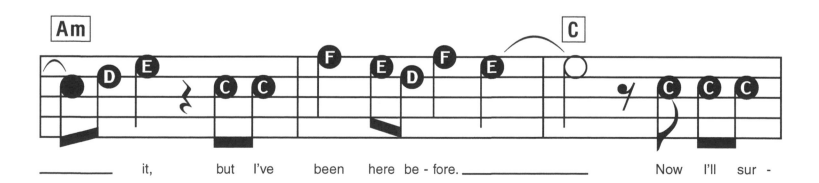

___ it, but I've been here be - fore. ___ Now I'll sur -

D.S. al Coda
(Return to %
Play to ⊕ and
Skip to Coda)

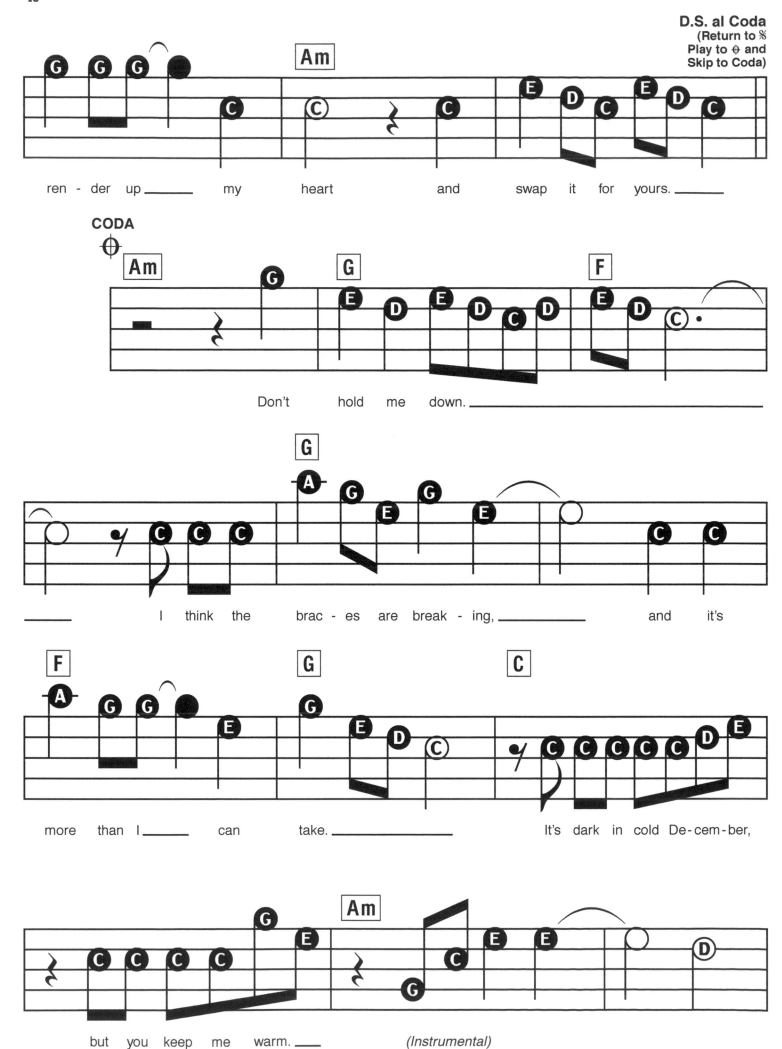

ren - der up _____ my heart and swap it for yours. _____

CODA

Don't hold me down. _____

_____ I think the brac - es are break - ing, _____ and it's

more than I _____ can take. _____ It's dark in cold De - cem - ber,

but you keep me warm. ___ *(Instrumental)*

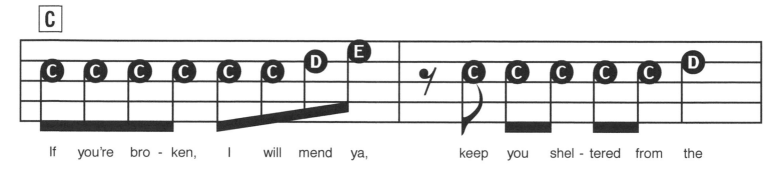

If you're bro - ken, I will mend ya, keep you shel - tered from the

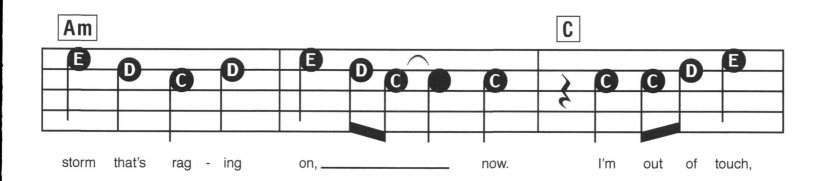

storm that's rag - ing on, _____ now. I'm out of touch,

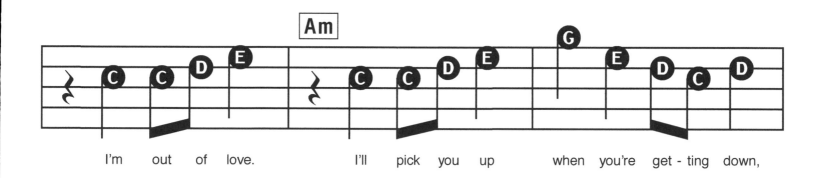

I'm out of love. I'll pick you up when you're get - ting down,

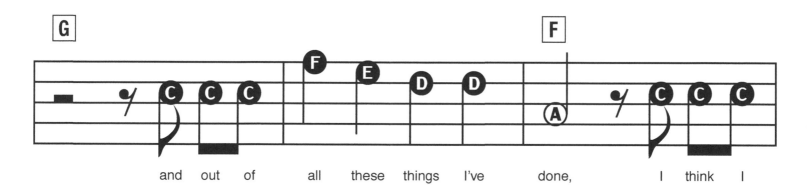

and out of all these things I've done, I think I

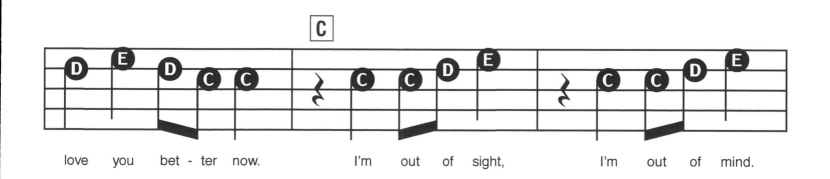

love you bet - ter now. I'm out of sight, I'm out of mind.

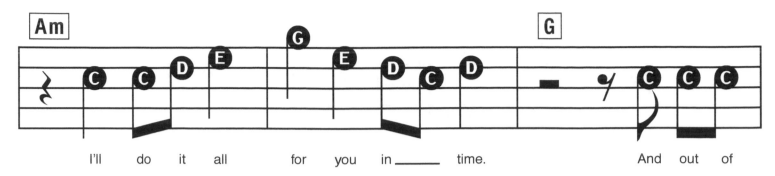

I'll do it all for you in _____ time. And out of

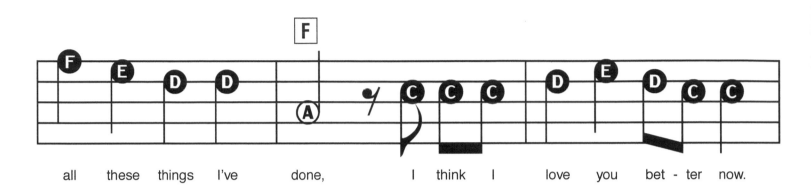

all these things I've done, I think I love you bet - ter now.

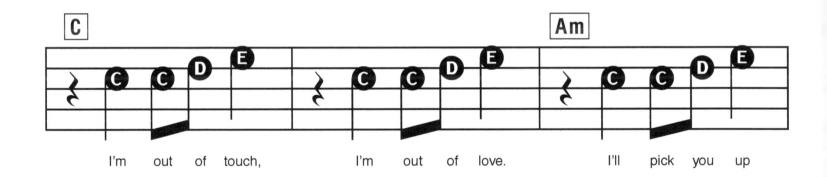

I'm out of touch, I'm out of love. I'll pick you up

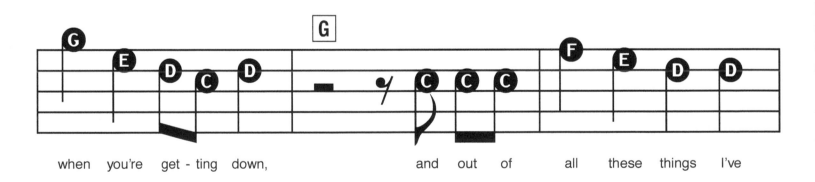

when you're get - ting down, and out of all these things I've

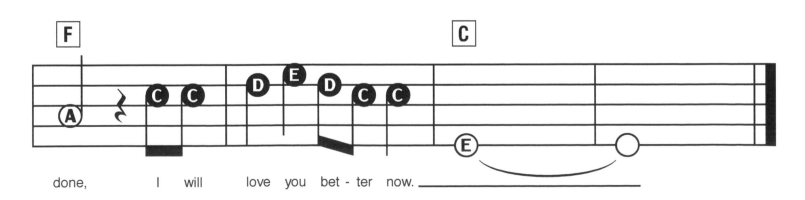

done, I will love you bet - ter now. _____

Perfect

Registration 4
Rhythm: Slow Rock or 6/8 March

Words and Music by
Ed Sheeran

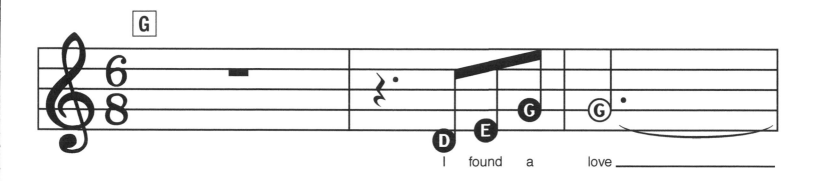

I found a love _____

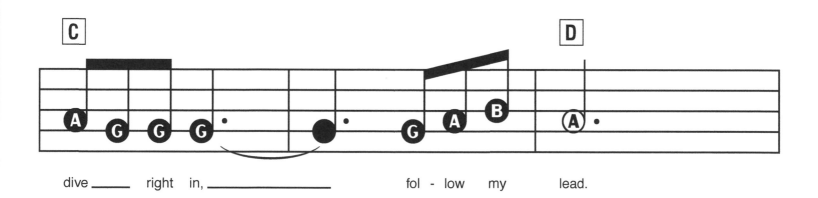

_____ for _____ me. _____ Dar - ling, just

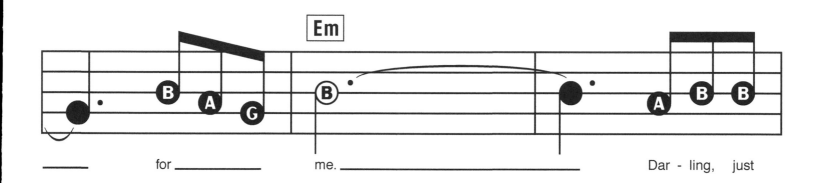

dive _____ right in, _____ fol - low my lead.

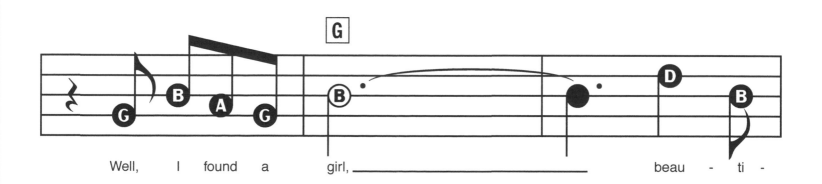

Well, I found a girl, _____ beau - ti -

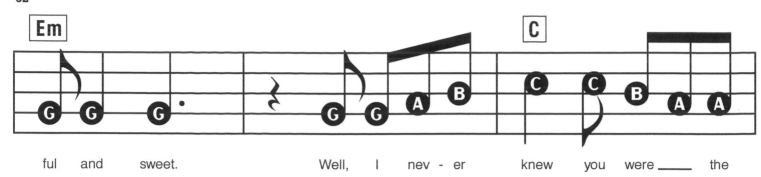

ful and sweet. Well, I nev - er knew you were ___ the

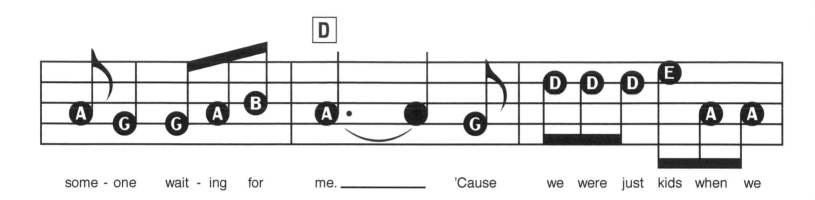

some - one wait - ing for me. ___ 'Cause we were just kids when we

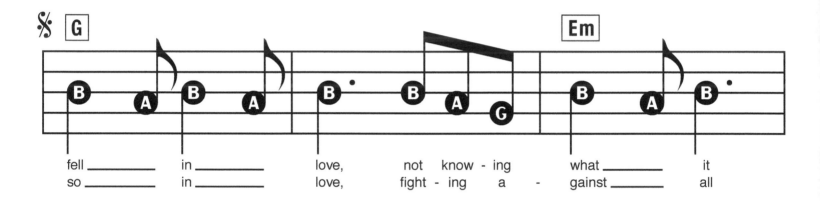

fell ___ in ___ love, not know - ing what ___ it
so ___ in ___ love, fight - ing a - gainst ___ all

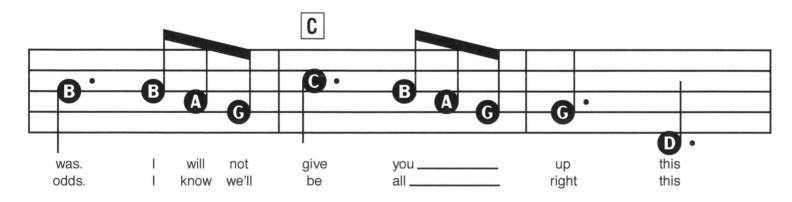

was. I will not give you ___ up this
odds. I know we'll be all ___ right this

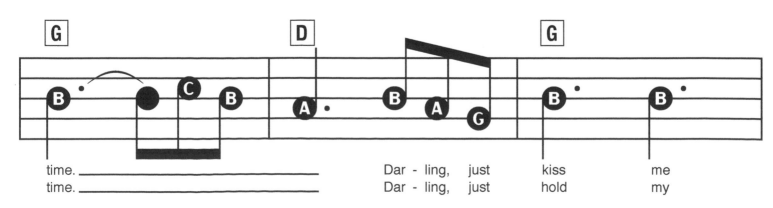

time. ___ Dar - ling, just kiss me
time. ___ Dar - ling, just hold my

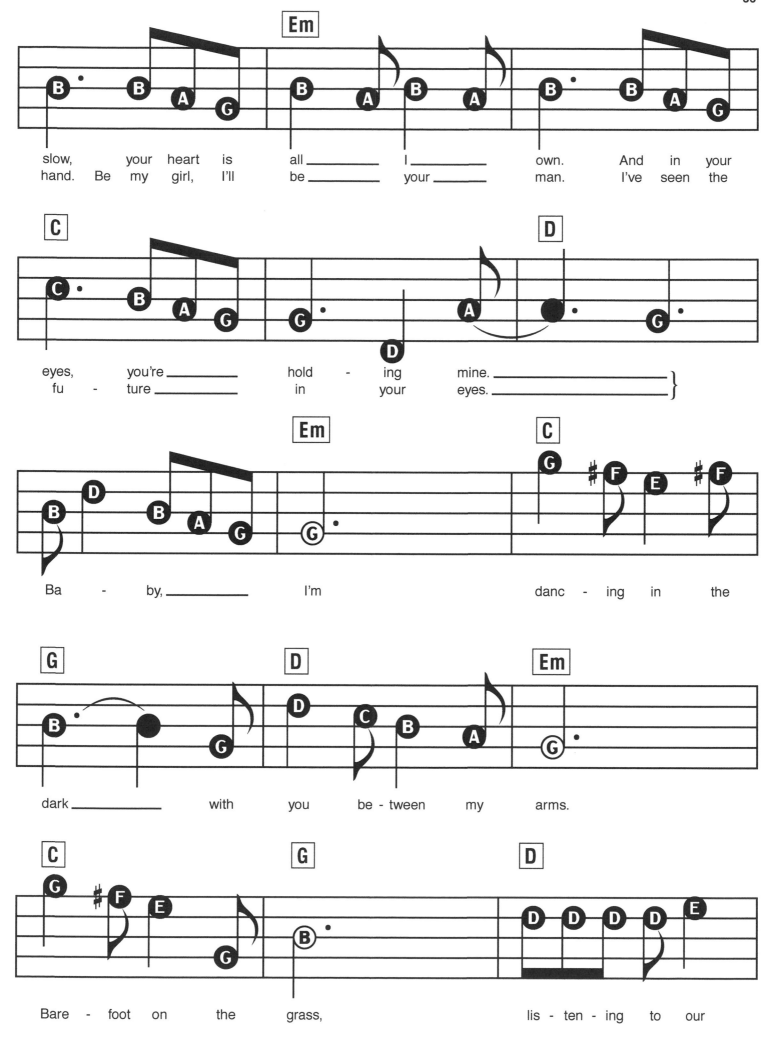

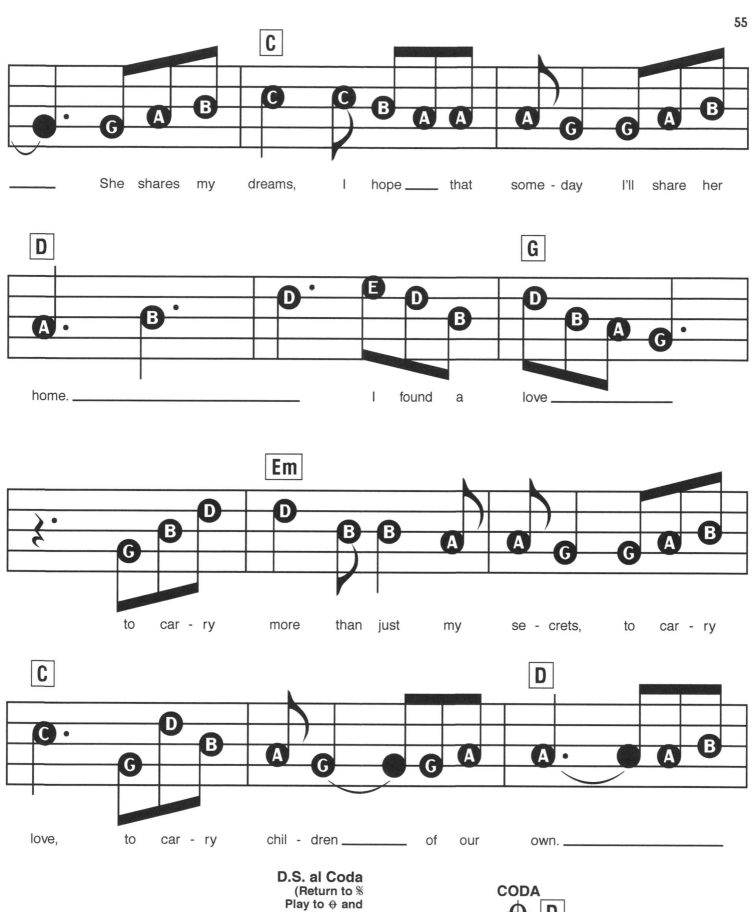

She shares my dreams, I hope ___ that some-day I'll share her

home. ___ I found a love ___

to car-ry more than just my se-crets, to car-ry

love, to car-ry chil-dren ___ of our own. ___

D.S. al Coda
(Return to 𝄋
Play to ⊕ and
Skip to Coda)

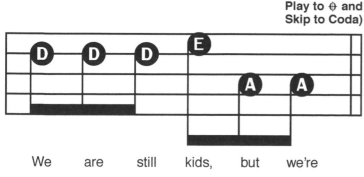

We are still kids, but we're

CODA
⊕ D

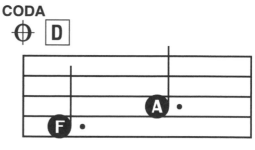

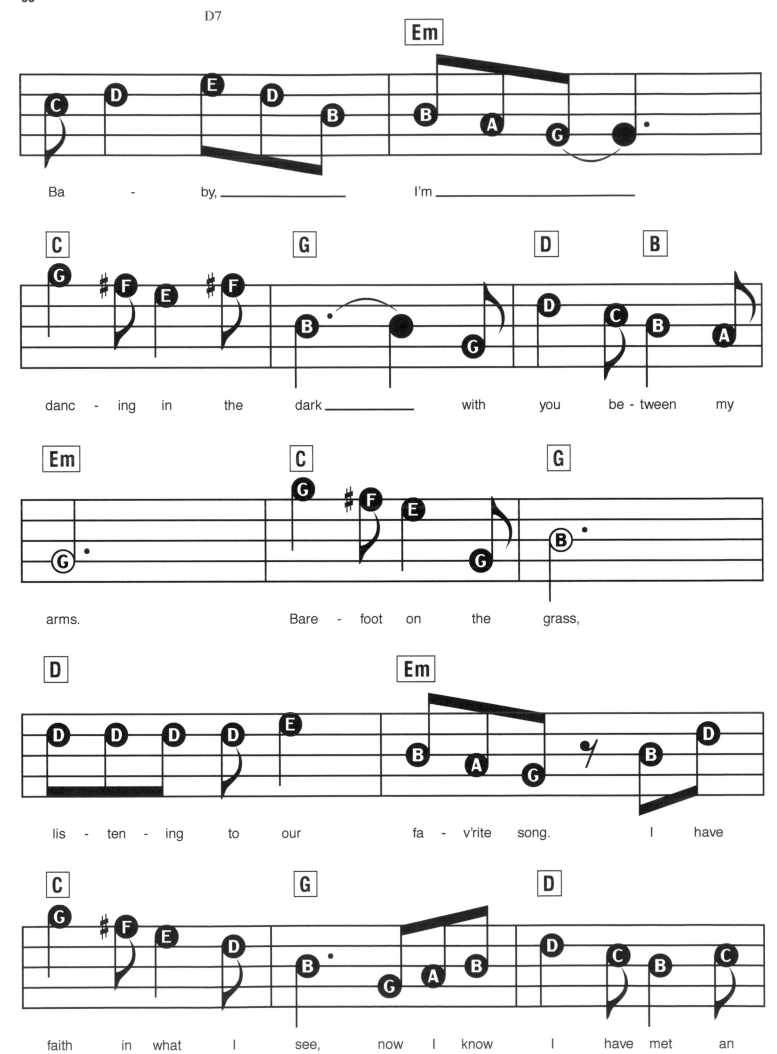

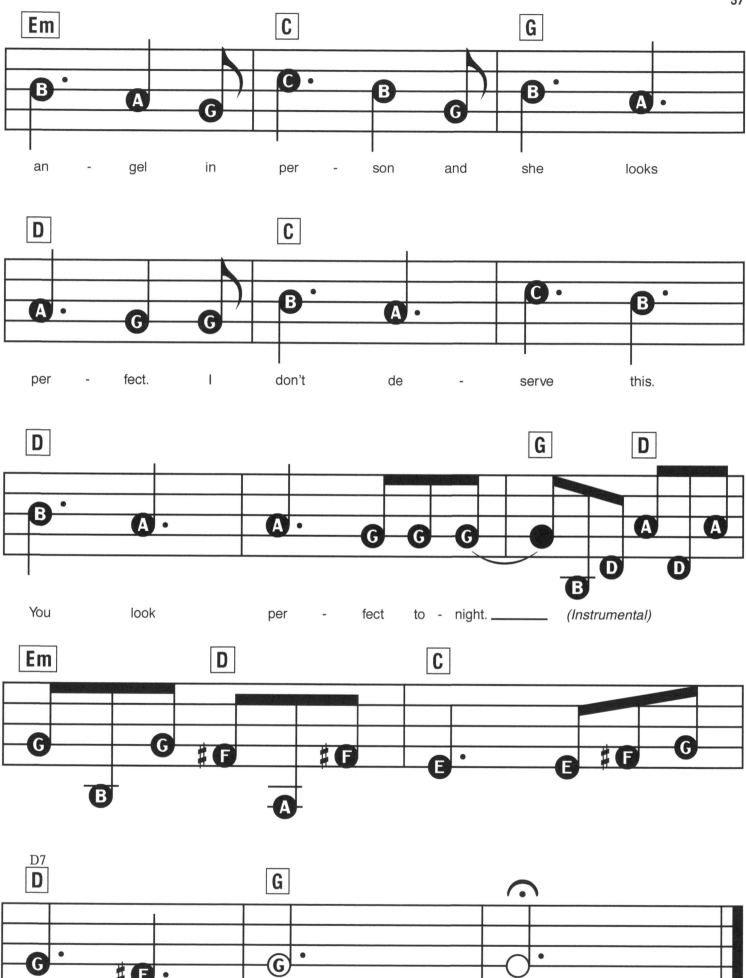

an - gel in per - son and she looks

per - fect. I don't de - serve this.

You look per - fect to - night. _____ (Instrumental)

Photograph

Registration 4
Rhythm: Rock or Folk

Words and Music by Ed Sheeran,
Johnny McDaid, Martin Peter Harrington
and Tom Leonard

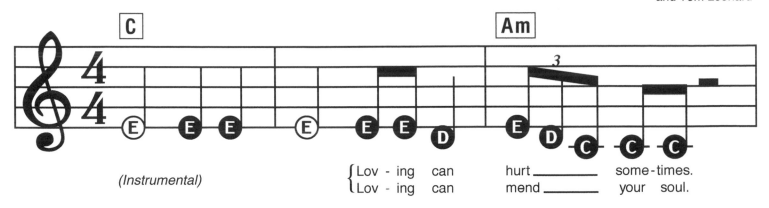

(Instrumental)

Lov - ing can hurt _____ some - times.
Lov - ing can mend _____ your soul.

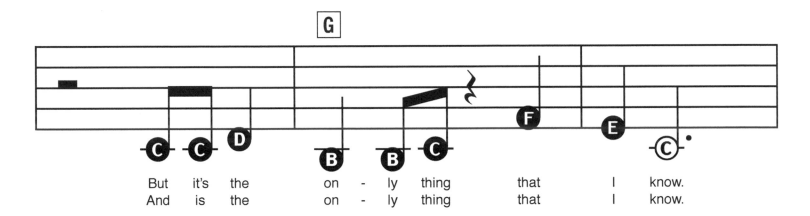

But it's the on - ly thing that I know.
And is the on - ly thing that I know.

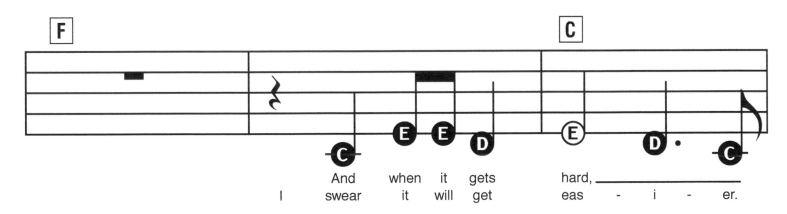

And when it gets hard, _____
I swear it will get eas - i - er.

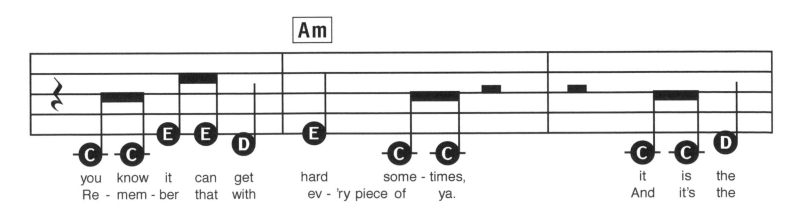

you know it can get hard some - times,
Re - mem - ber that with ev - 'ry piece of ya.

it is the
And it's the

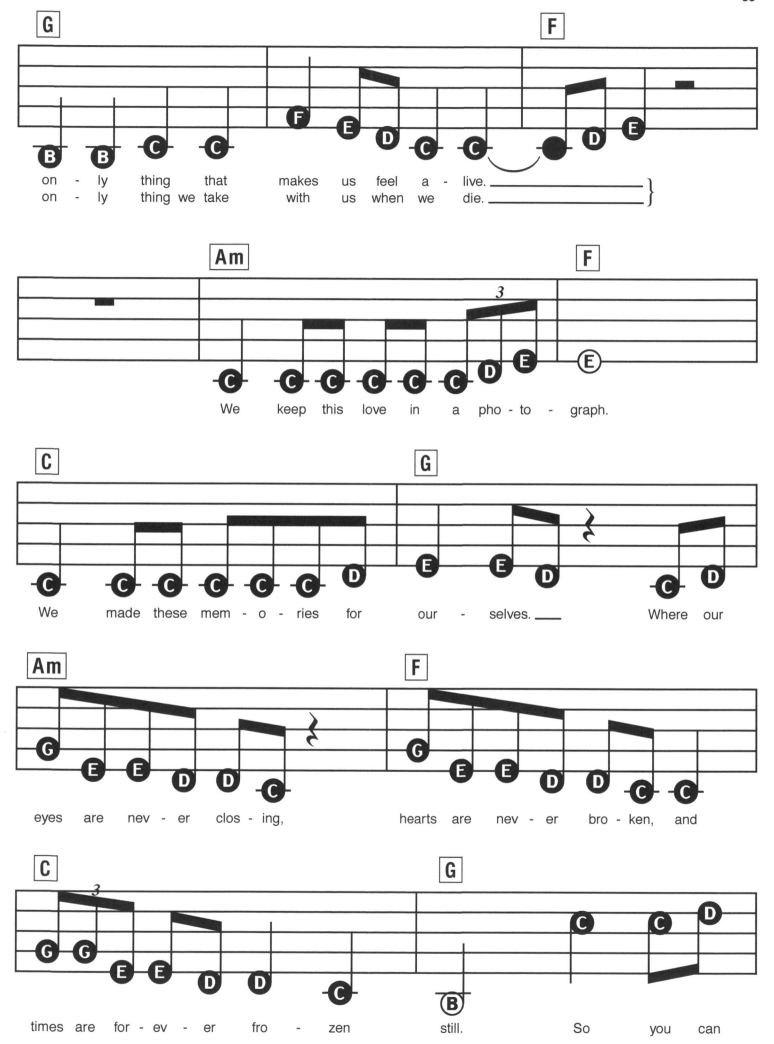

59

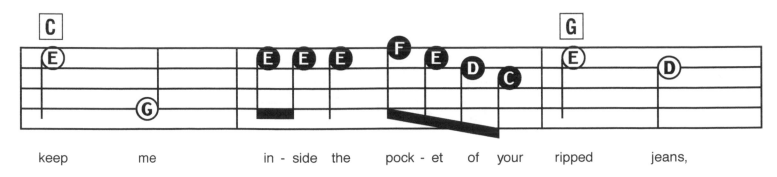

keep   me   in - side the   pock - et   of   your   ripped   jeans,

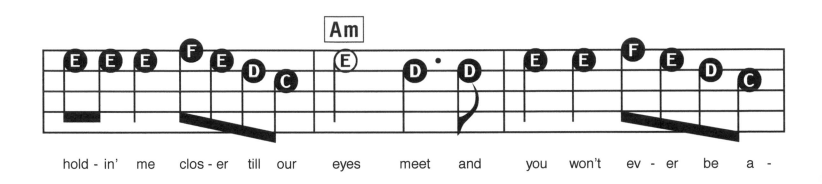

hold - in' me   clos - er   till   our   eyes   meet   and   you   won't   ev - er   be   a -

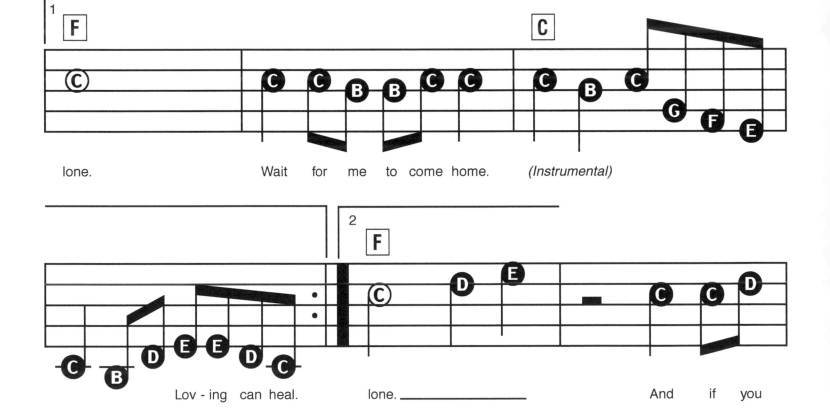

lone.   Wait   for   me   to   come   home.   *(Instrumental)*

Lov - ing can heal.   lone. _____   And   if   you

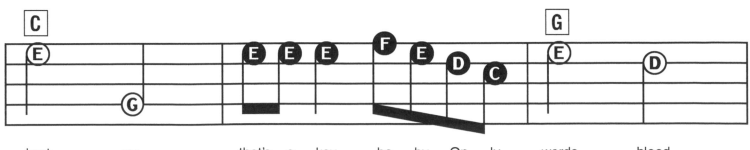

hurt   me,   that's   o - kay,   ba - by.   On - ly   words   bleed.

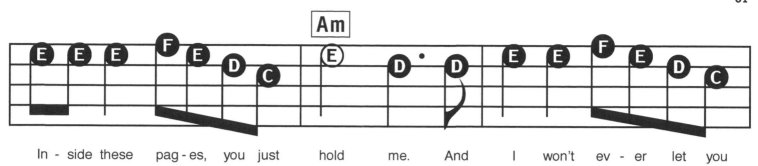

In - side these pag - es, you just hold me. And I won't ev - er let you

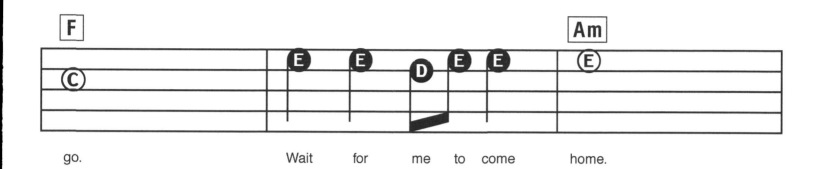

go. Wait for me to come home.

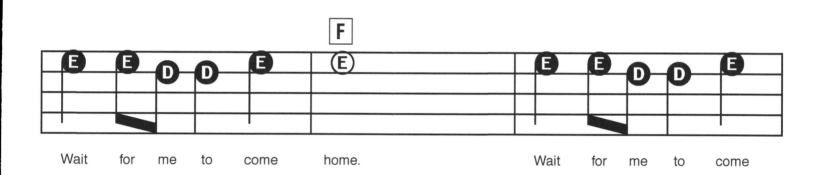

Wait for me to come home. Wait for me to come

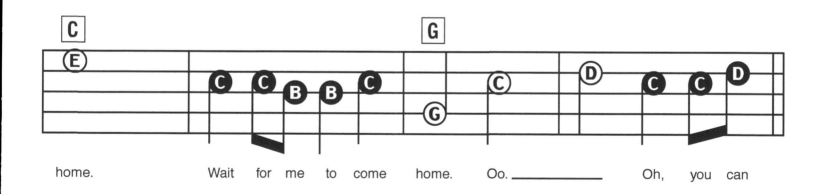

home. Wait for me to come home. Oo. _____ Oh, you can

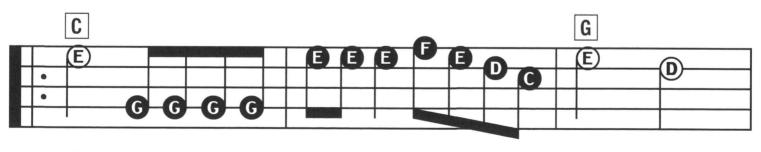

fit me in - side the neck - lace you got when you were six - teen,
hurt me, well, that's o - kay, ba - by. On - ly words bleed.

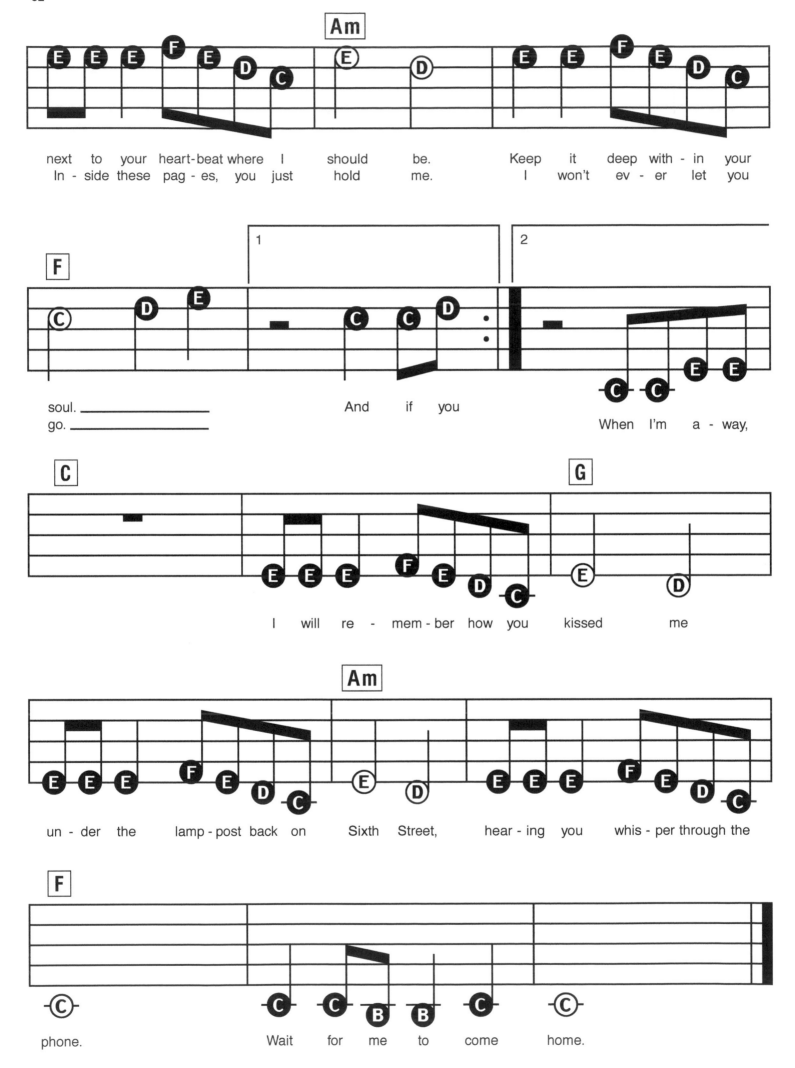

Shape of You

Registration 5
Rhythm: Pop or Techno

Words and Music by Ed Sheeran,
Kevin Briggs, Kandi Burruss, Tameka Cottle,
Steve Mac and Johnny McDaid

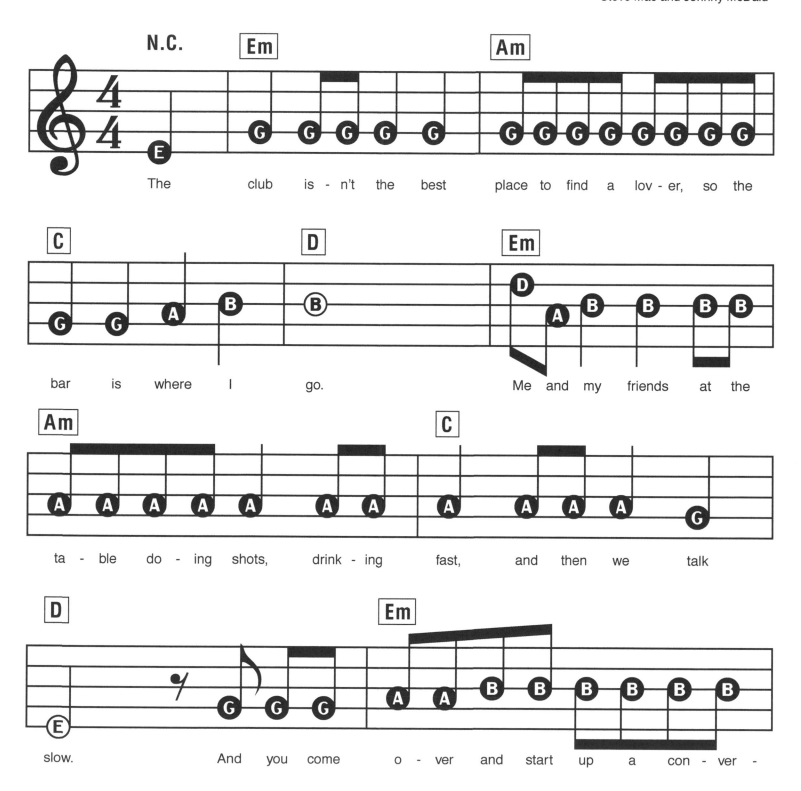

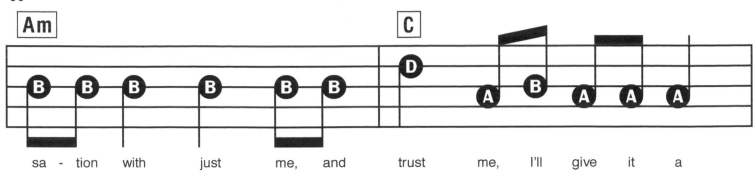

sa - tion with just me, and trust me, I'll give it a

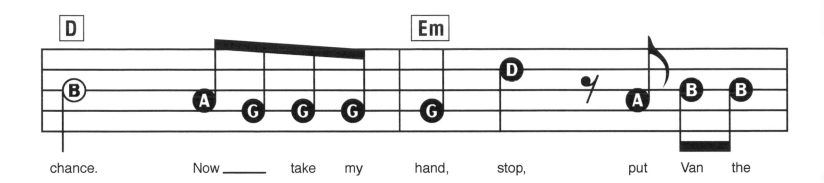

chance. Now _____ take my hand, stop, put Van the

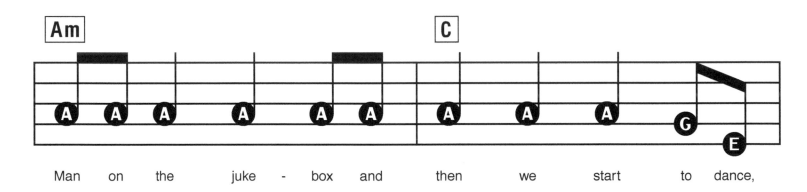

Man on the juke - box and then we start to dance,

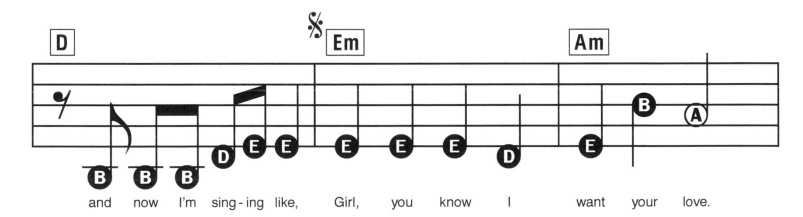

and now I'm sing - ing like, Girl, you know I want your love.

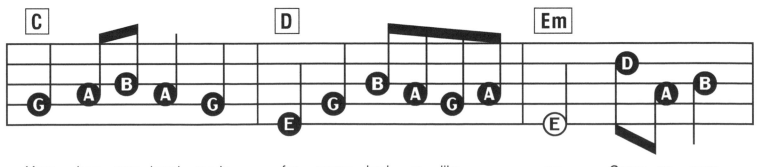

Your love was hand - made for some - bod - y like _____ me. Come on, now,

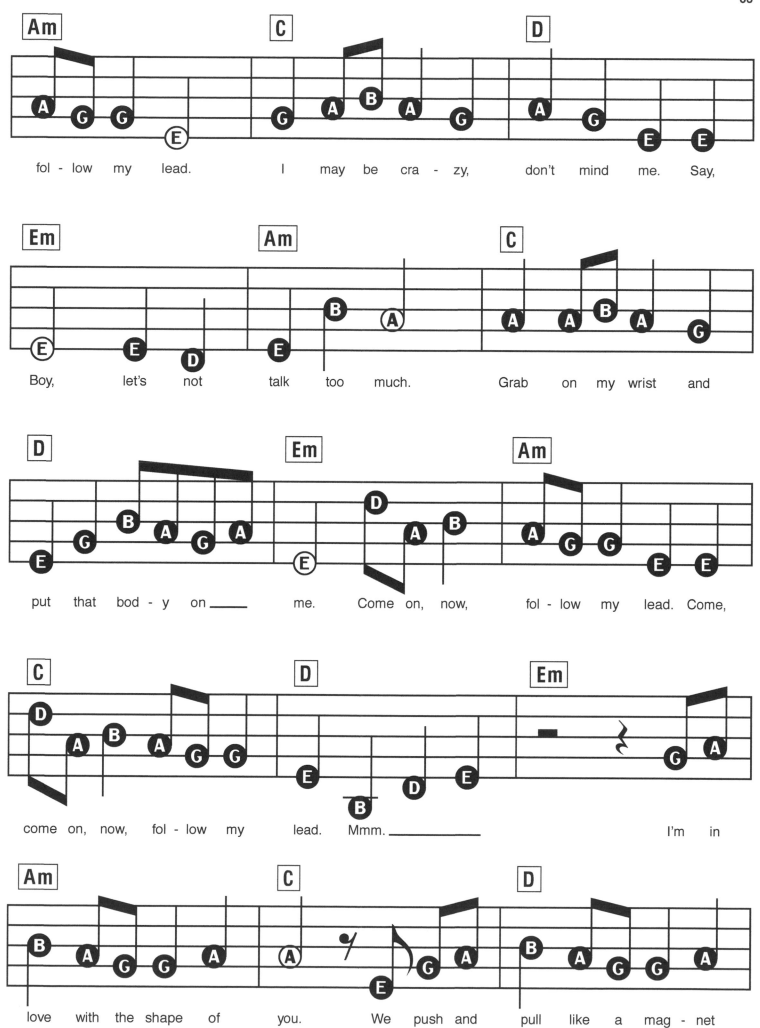

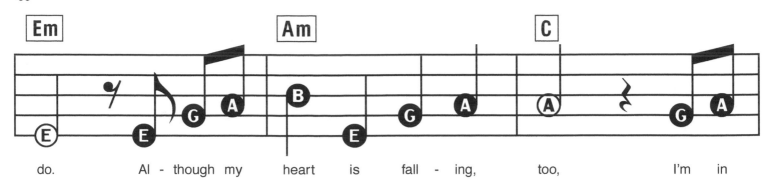

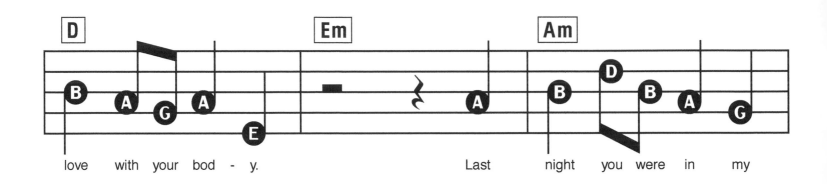

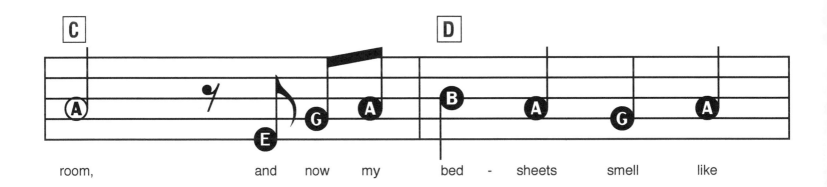

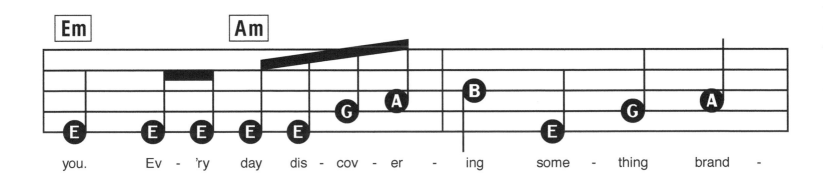

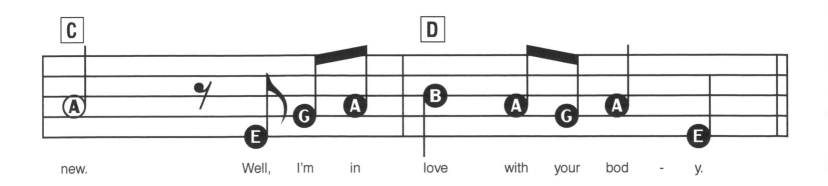

67

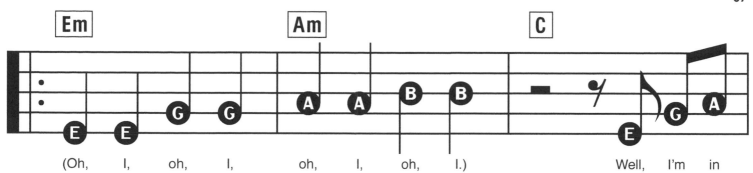

(Oh,   I,   oh,   I,   oh,   I,   oh,   I.)   Well,   I'm   in

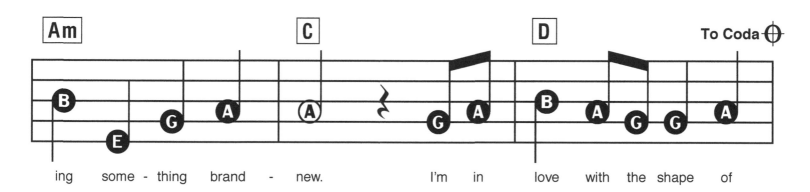

love   with   your   bod   -   y.   Ev - 'ry   day   dis - cov - er -

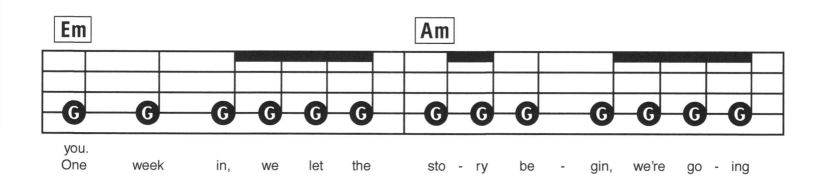

ing   some - thing   brand - new.   I'm   in   love   with   the   shape   of

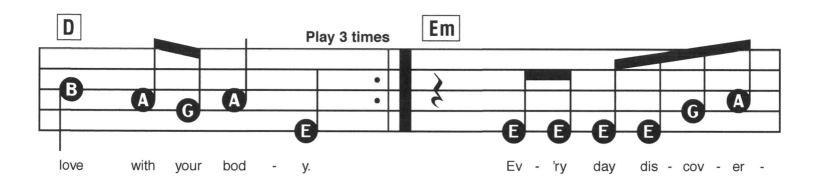

you.
One   week   in,   we   let   the   sto - ry   be - gin,   we're   go - ing

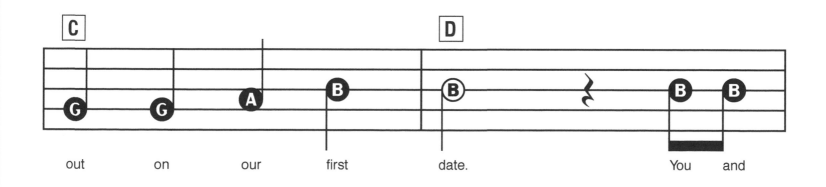

out   on   our   first   date.   You   and

68

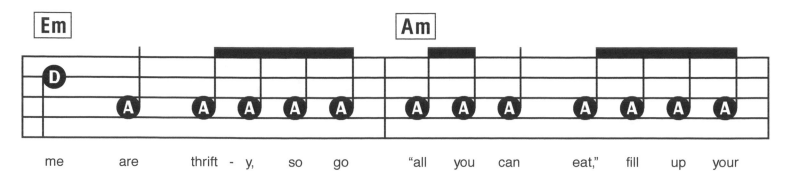

me are thrift - y, so go "all you can eat," fill up your

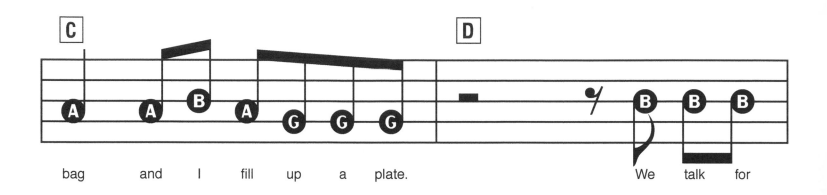

bag and I fill up a plate. We talk for

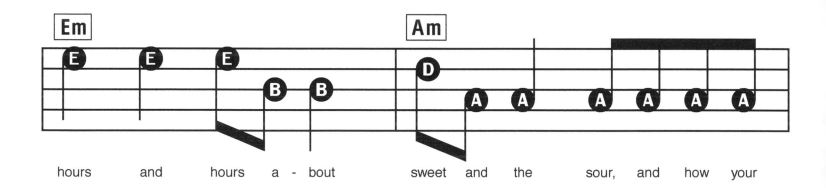

hours and hours a - bout sweet and the sour, and how your

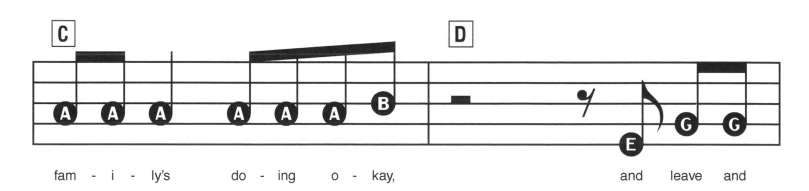

fam - i - ly's do - ing o - kay, and leave and

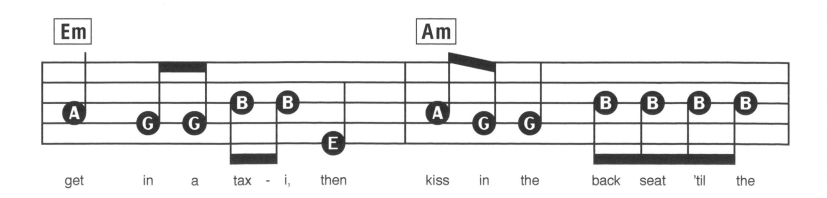

get in a tax - i, then kiss in the back seat 'til the

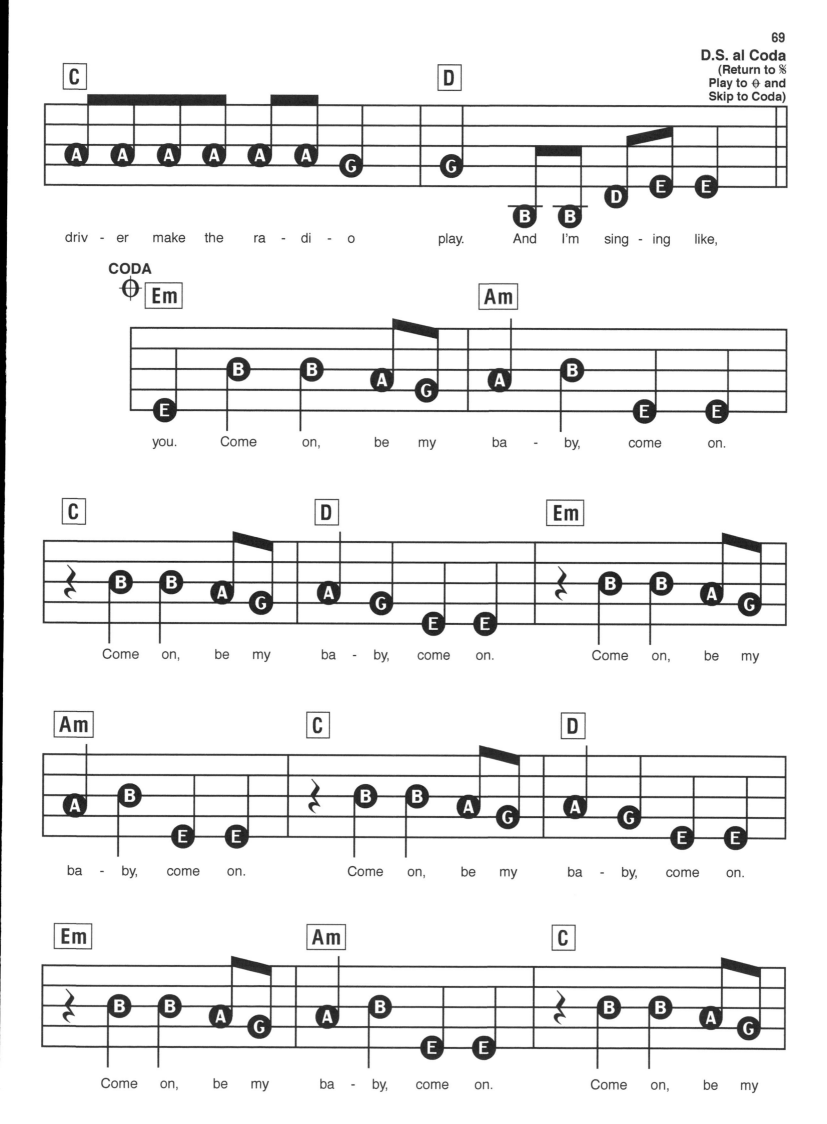

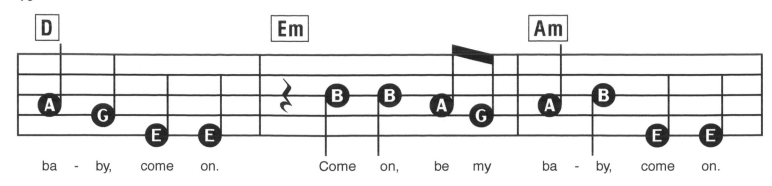

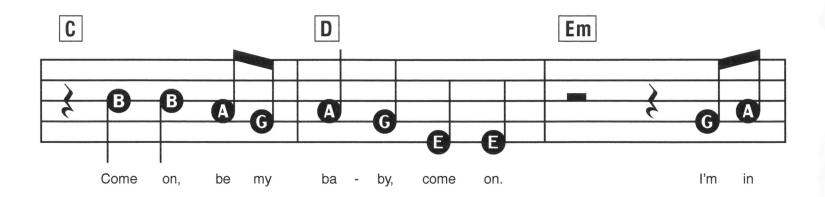

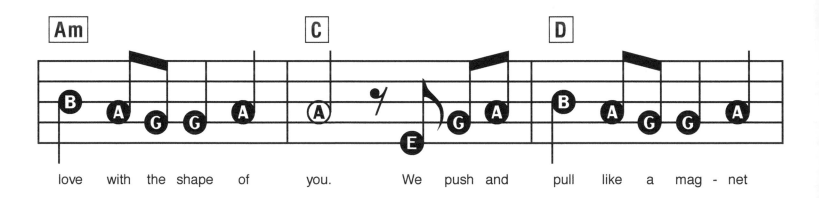

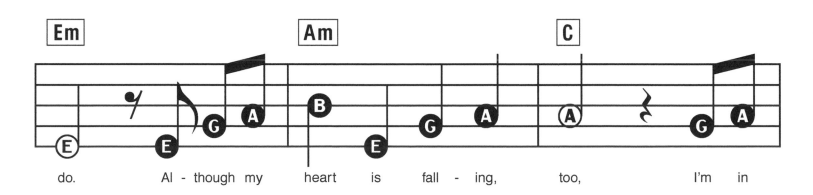

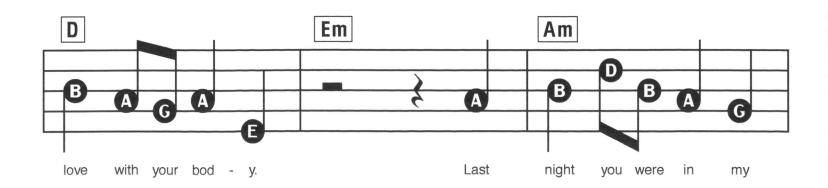

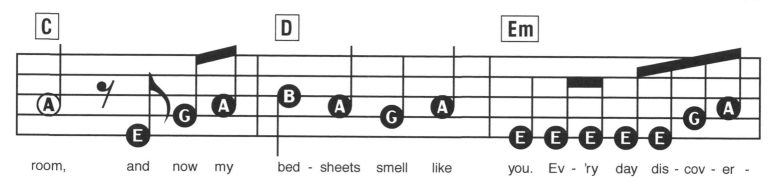

room, and now my bed-sheets smell like you. Ev - 'ry day dis - cov - er -

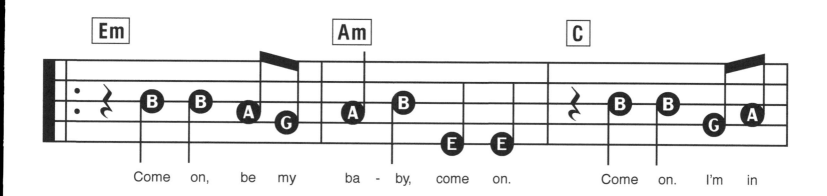

ing some - thing brand - new. Well, I'm in love with your bod - y.

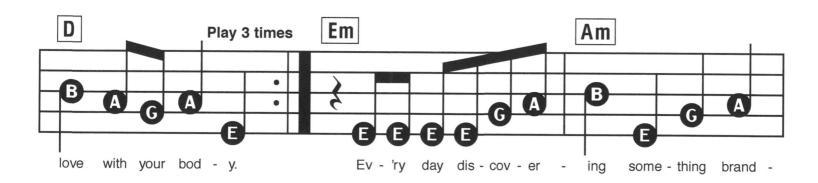

Come on, be my ba - by, come on. Come on. I'm in

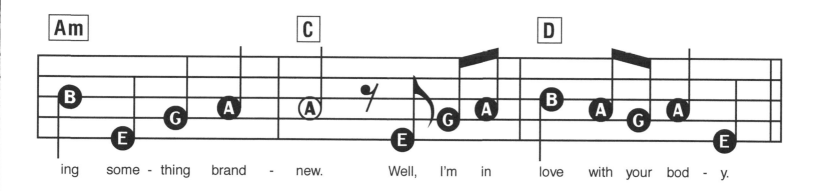

Play 3 times

love with your bod - y. Ev - 'ry day dis - cov - er - ing some - thing brand -

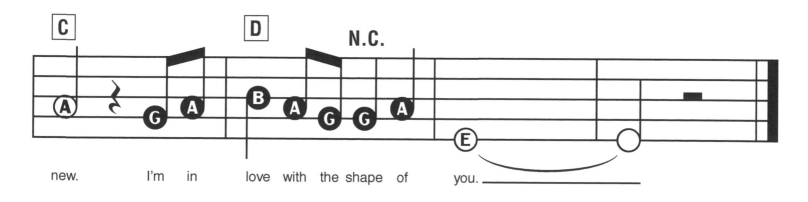

N.C.

new. I'm in love with the shape of you. _____

Sing

Registration 4
Rhythm: Rock

Words and Music by Ed Sheeran
and Pharrell Williams

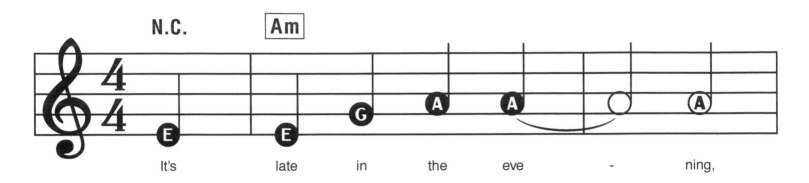

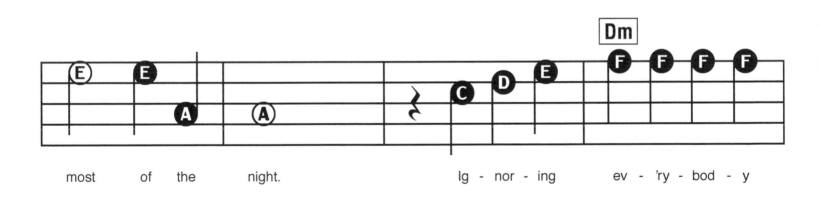

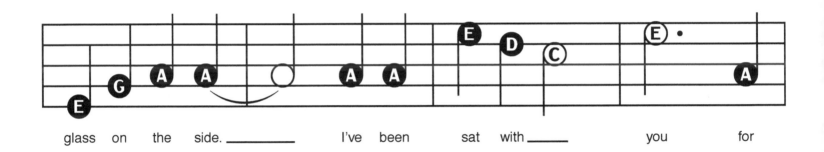

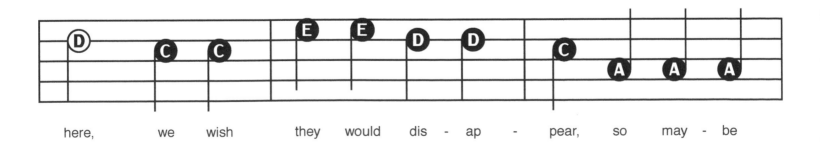

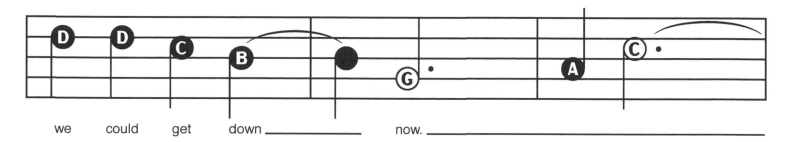

we could get down _____ now. _____

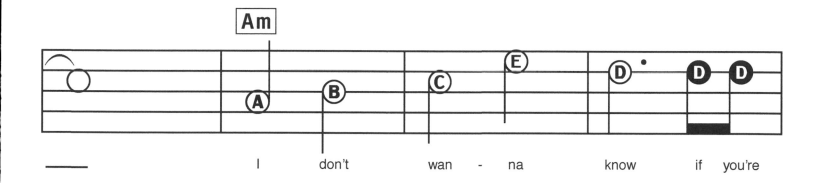

Am

_____ I don't wan - na know if you're

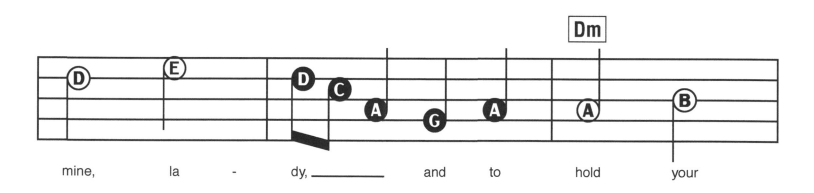

get - ting a - head of the pro - gram. I want you to _____ be

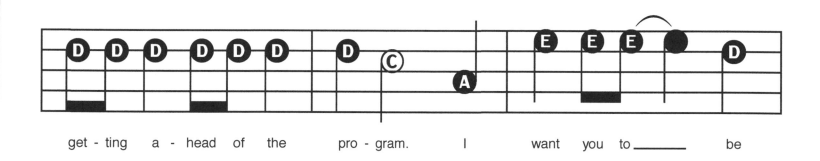

Dm

mine, la - dy, _____ and to hold your

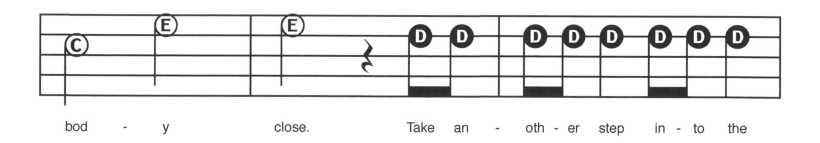

bod - y close. Take an - oth - er step in - to the

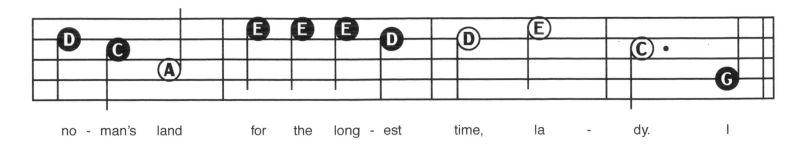

no - man's land for the long - est time, la - dy. I

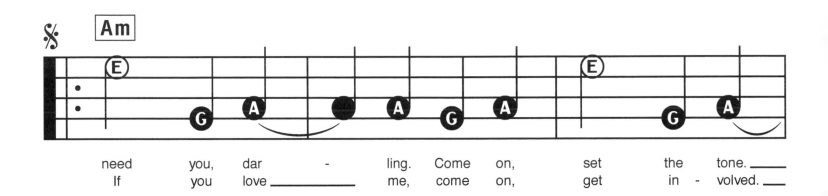

need you, dar - ling. Come on, set the tone. _____
If you love _____ me, come on, get in - volved. ___

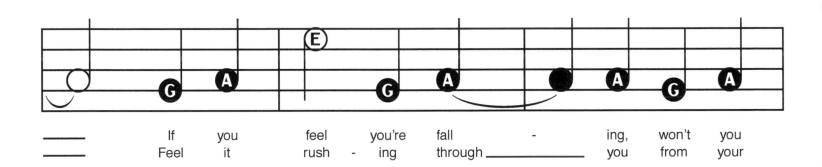

_____ If you feel you're fall - ing, won't you
_____ Feel it rush - ing through _____ you from your

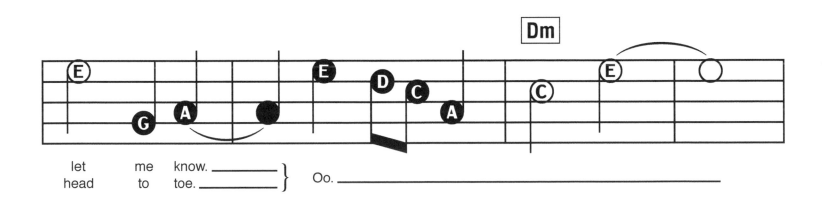

let me know. _____ } Oo. _____
head to toe. _____

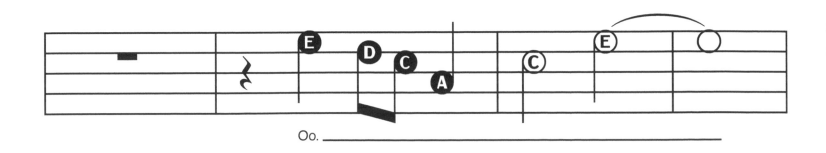

Oo. _____

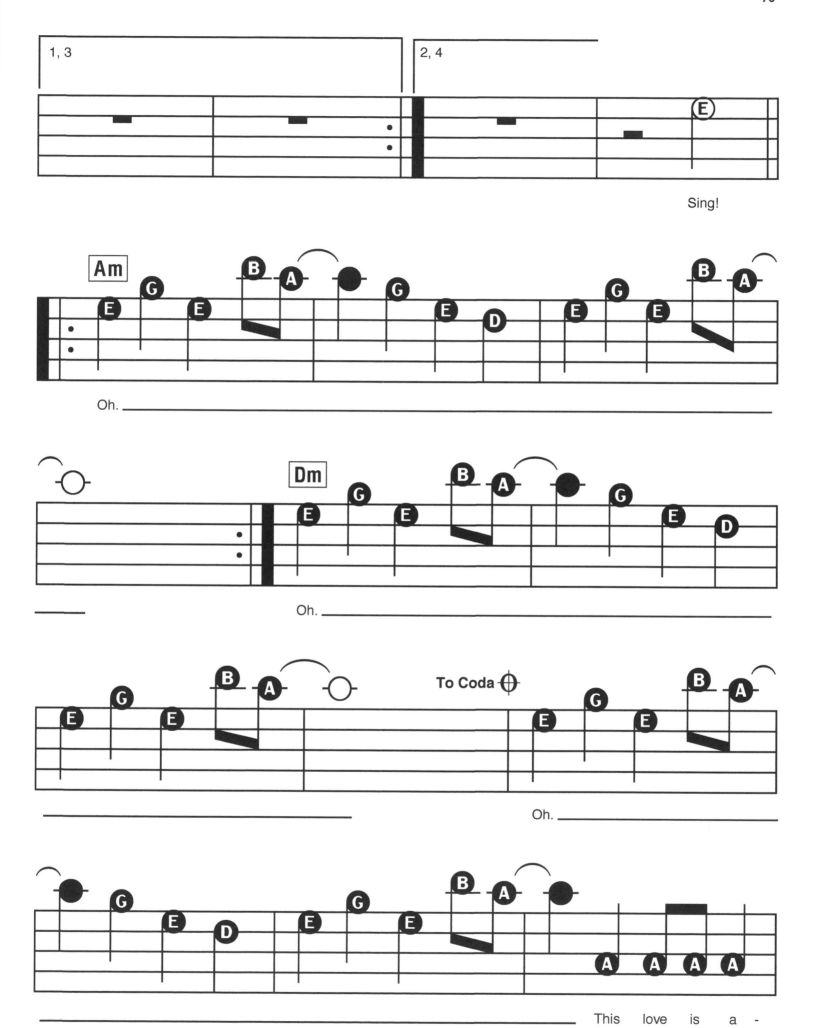

Am

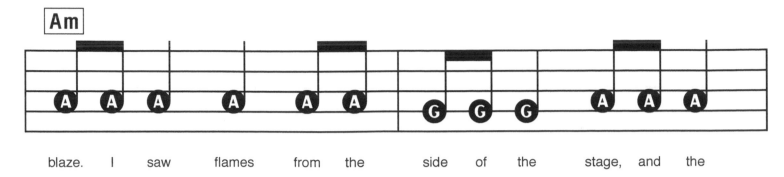

blaze. I saw flames from the side of the stage, and the

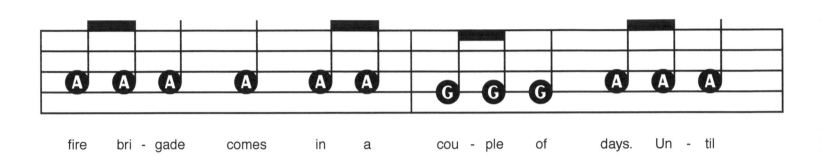

fire bri - gade comes in a cou - ple of days. Un - til

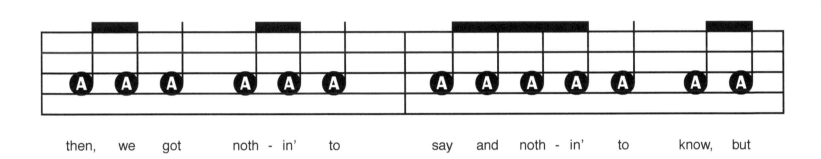

then, we got noth - in' to say and noth - in' to know, but

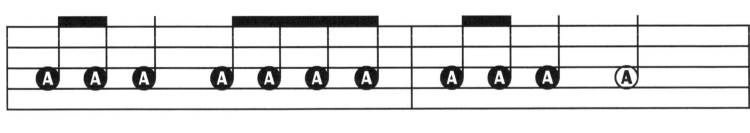

some - thin' to drink and may - be some - thin' to smoke.

Dm

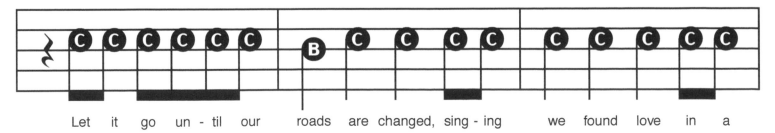

Let it go un - til our roads are changed, sing - ing we found love in a

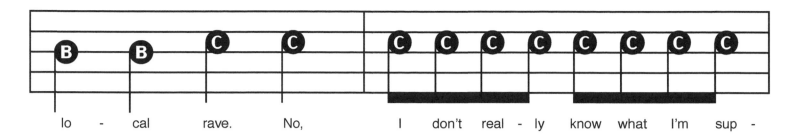

lo - cal rave. No, I don't real - ly know what I'm sup -

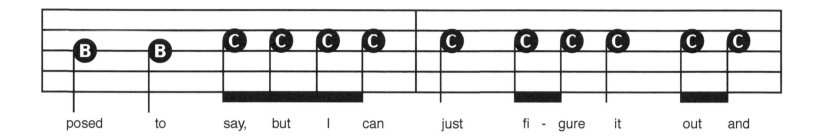

posed to say, but I can just fi - gure it out and

Am

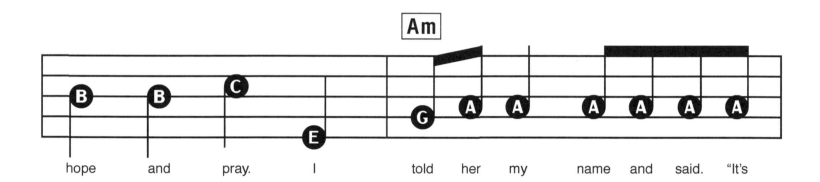

hope and pray. I told her my name and said. "It's

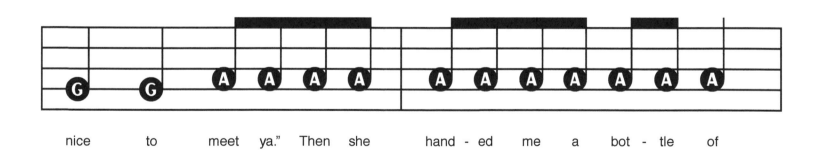

nice to meet ya." Then she hand - ed me a bot - tle of

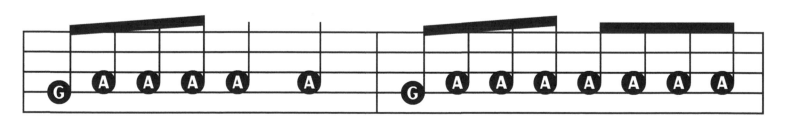

wa - ter with te - qui - la. I al - read - y know it, she's a

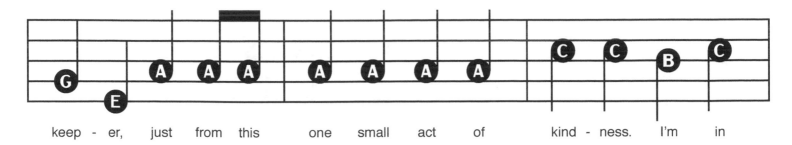

keep - er, just from this one small act of kind - ness. I'm in

Dm

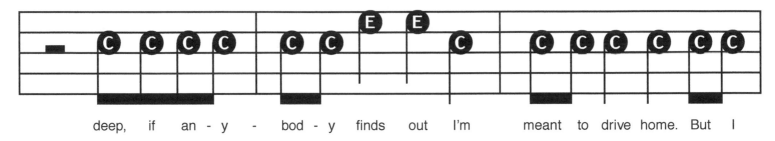

deep, if an - y - bod - y finds out I'm meant to drive home. But I

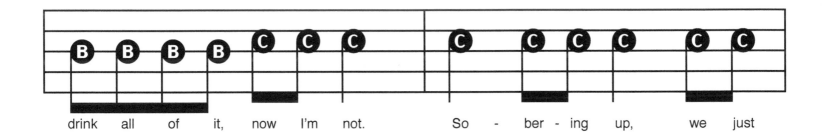

drink all of it, now I'm not. So - ber - ing up, we just

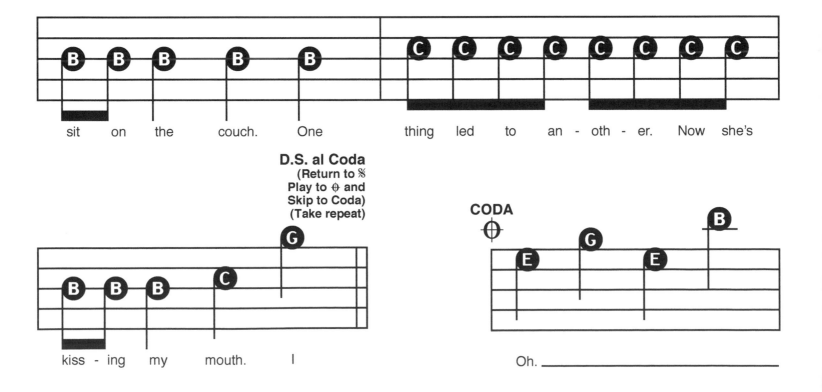

sit on the couch. One thing led to an - oth - er. Now she's

D.S. al Coda
(Return to 𝄋
Play to ⊕ and
Skip to Coda)
(Take repeat)

kiss - ing my mouth. I

CODA

Oh. _____

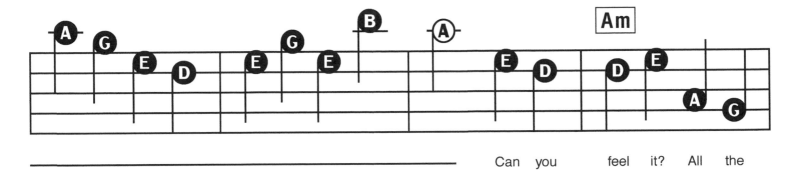

Can you feel it? All the

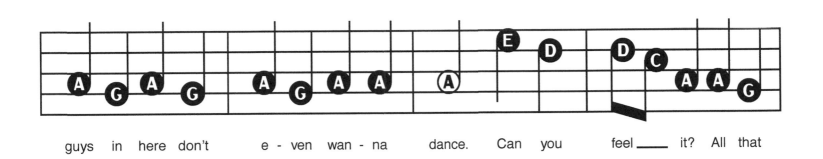

guys in here don't e - ven wan - na dance. Can you feel____ it? All that

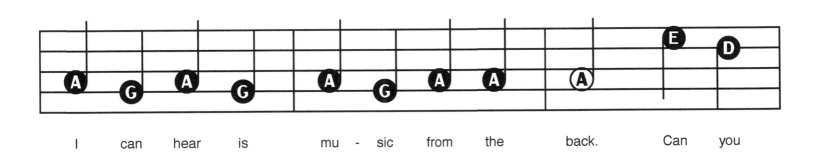

I can hear is mu - sic from the back. Can you

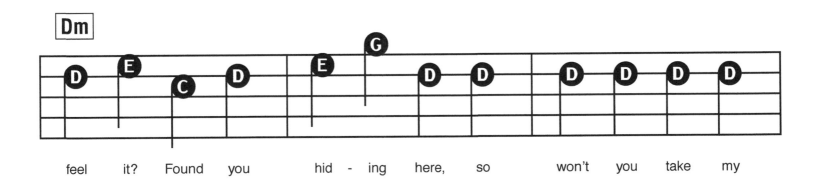

feel it? Found you hid - ing here, so won't you take my

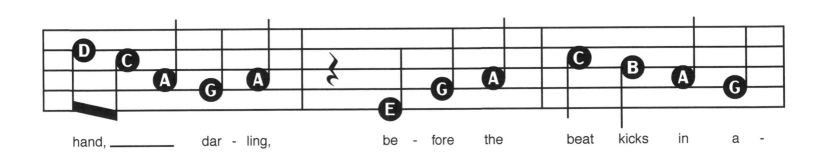

hand,_____ dar - ling, be - fore the beat kicks in a -

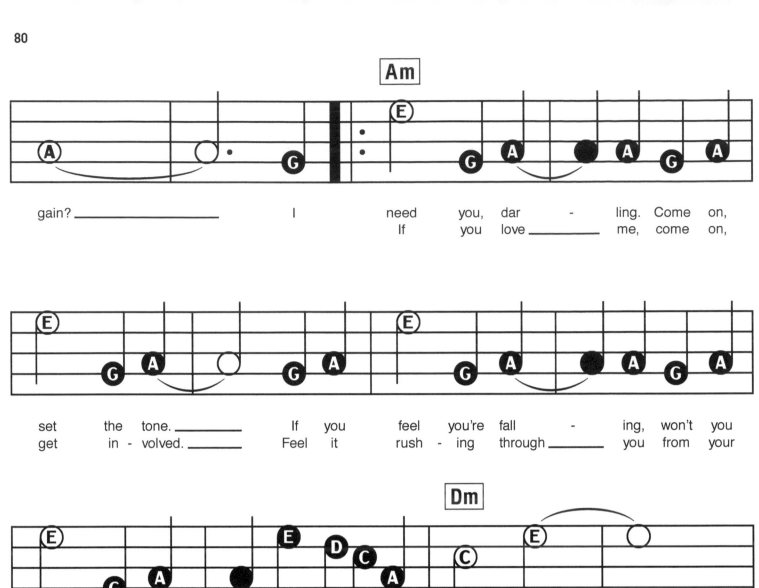

gain? _____ I need you, dar - ling. Come on,
If you love _____ me, come on,

set the tone. _____ If you feel you're fall - ing, won't you
get in - volved. _____ Feel it rush - ing through _____ you from your

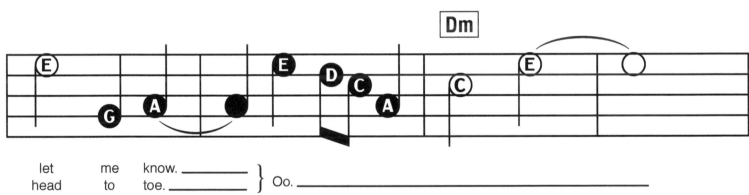

let me know. _____ ⎫
head to toe. _____ ⎬ Oo. _____

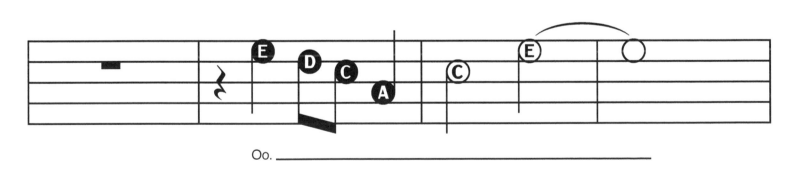

Oo. _____

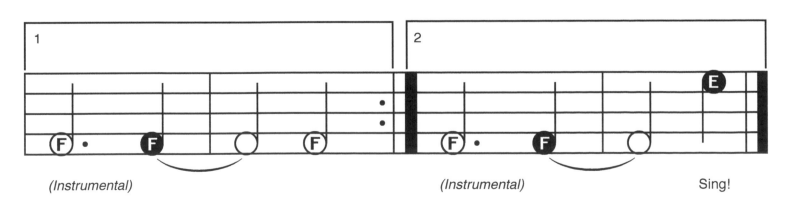

(Instrumental)   (Instrumental)   Sing!

Thinking Out Loud

Registration 4
Rhythm: 8-Beat or Rock

Words and Music by Ed Sheeran
and Amy Wadge

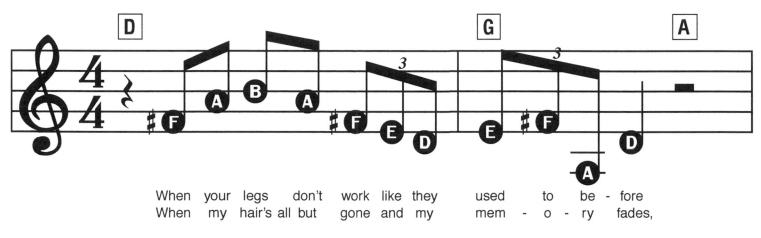

When your legs don't work like they used to be - fore
When my hair's all but gone and my mem - o - ry fades,

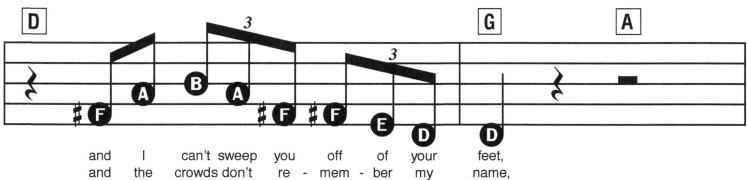

and I can't sweep you off of your feet,
and the crowds don't re - mem - ber my name,

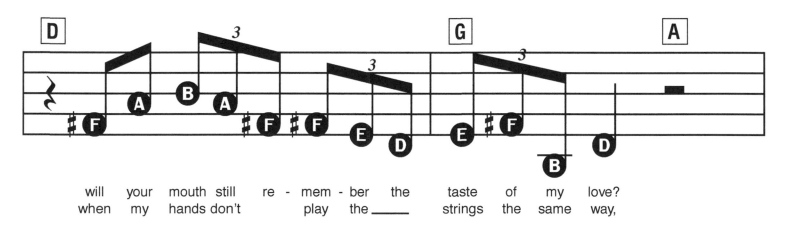

will your mouth still re - mem - ber the taste of my love?
when my hands don't play the _____ strings the same way,

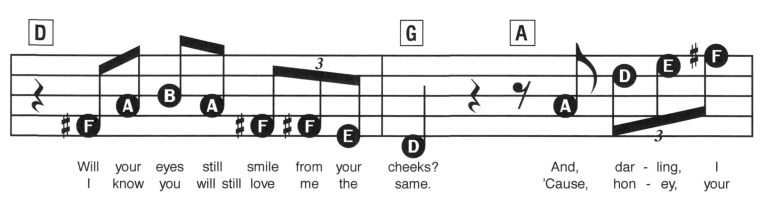

Will your eyes still smile from your cheeks? And, dar - ling, I
I know you will still love me the same. 'Cause, hon - ey, your

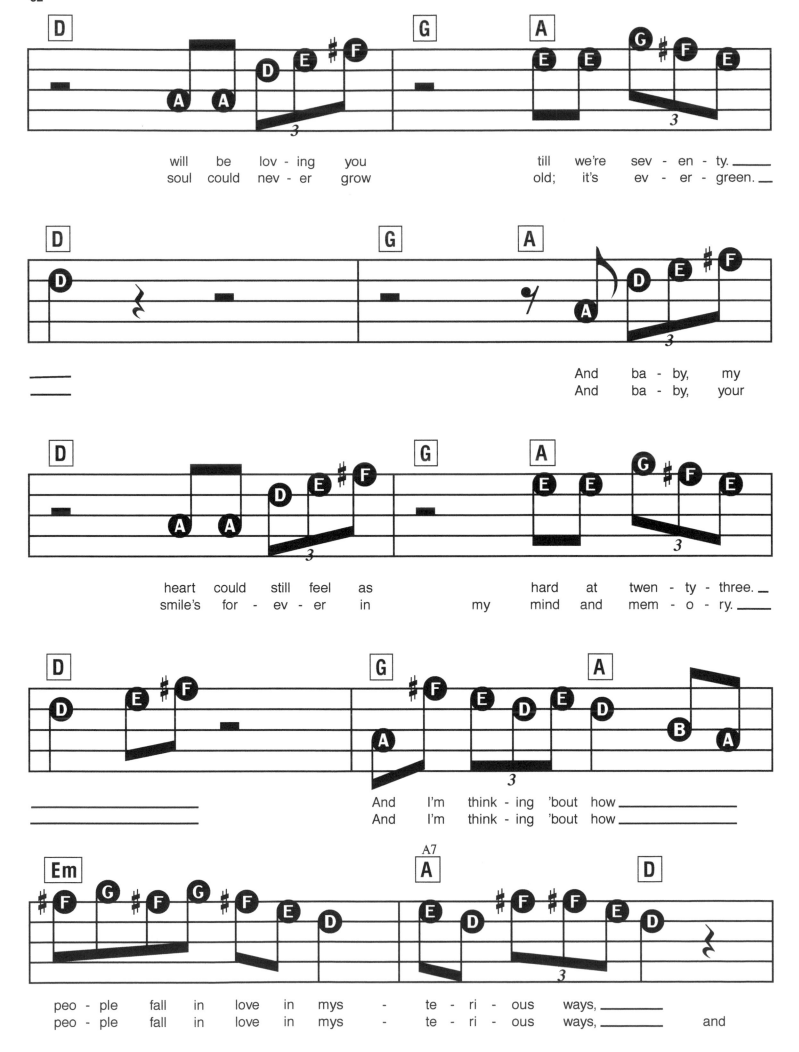

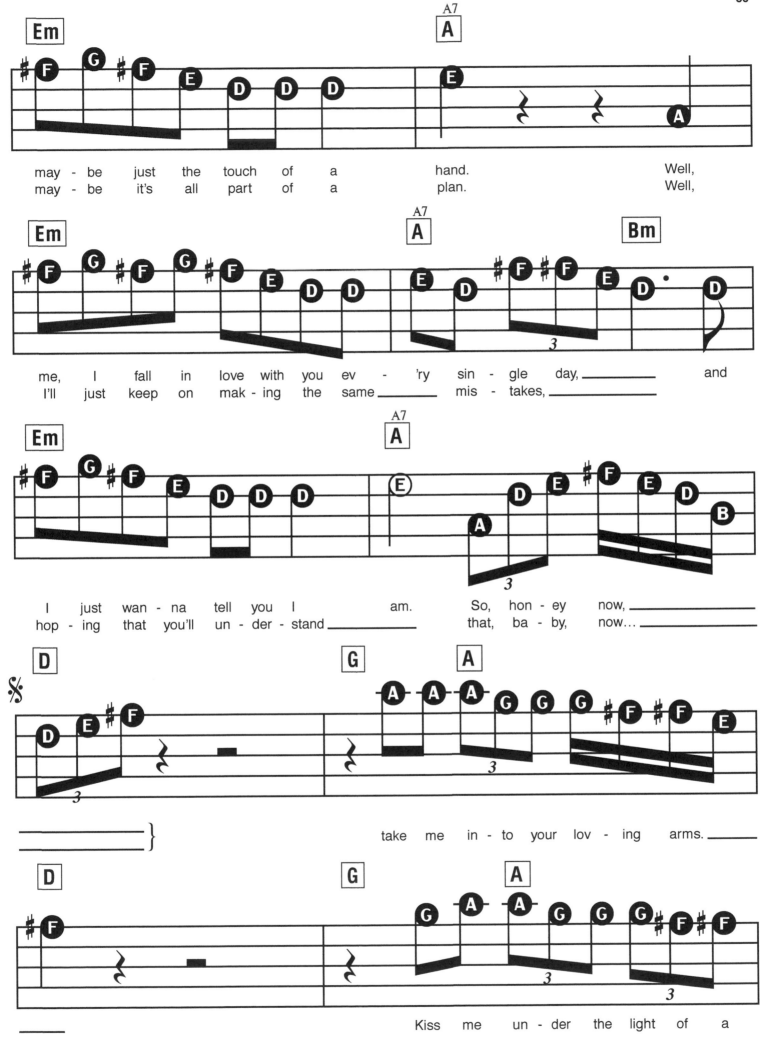

thou - sand stars. _____ Place your head on my beat - ing heart. ____

_____ I'm think - ing out _____ loud; _____ may - be

we found love right where we are.

2.

where we are.

(La, la,

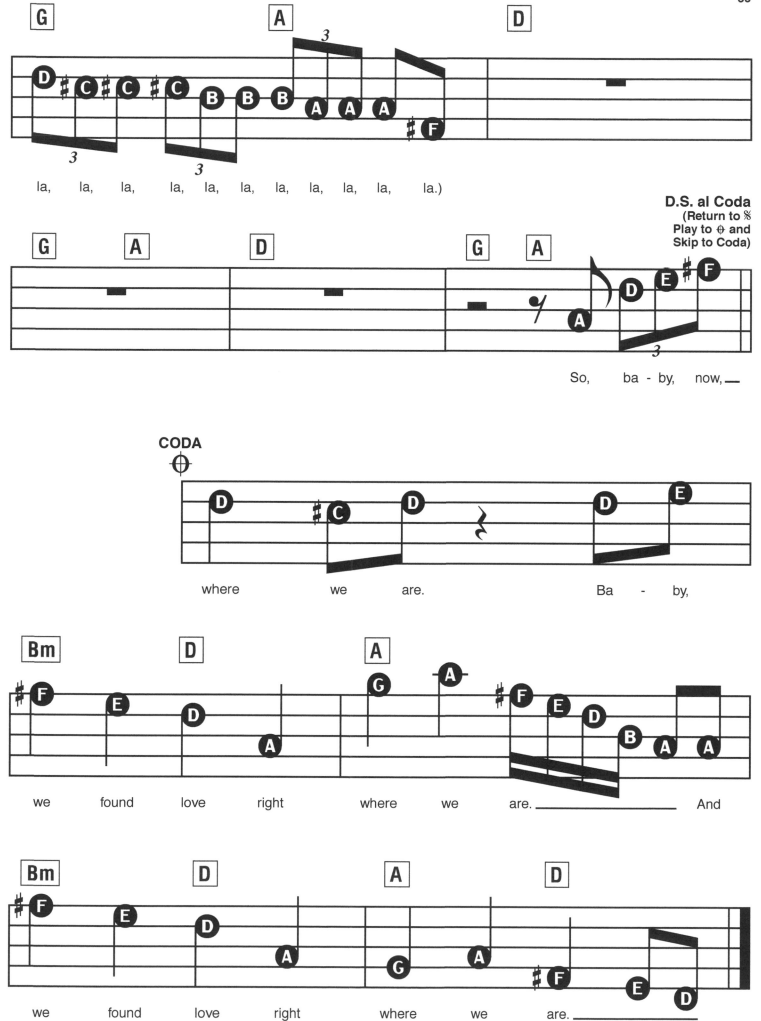

la, la, la, la, la, la, la, la, la, la, la.)

D.S. al Coda
(Return to %
Play to ⊕ and
Skip to Coda)

So, ba - by, now, ___

CODA

where we are. Ba - by,

we found love right where we are. ___ And

we found love right where we are. ___

Registration Guide

- Match the Registration number on the song to the corresponding numbered category below. Select and activate an instrumental sound available on your instrument.

- Choose an automatic rhythm appropriate to the mood and style of the song. (Consult your Owner's Guide for proper operation of automatic rhythm features.)

- Adjust the tempo and volume controls to comfortable settings.

Registration

1	Mellow	Flutes, Clarinet, Oboe, Flugel Horn, Trombone, French Horn, Organ Flutes
2	Ensemble	Brass Section, Sax Section, Wind Ensemble, Full Organ, Theater Organ
3	Strings	Violin, Viola, Cello, Fiddle, String Ensemble, Pizzicato, Organ Strings
4	Guitars	Acoustic/Electric Guitars, Banjo, Mandolin, Dulcimer, Ukulele, Hawaiian Guitar
5	Mallets	Vibraphone, Marimba, Xylophone, Steel Drums, Bells, Celesta, Chimes
6	Liturgical	Pipe Organ, Hand Bells, Vocal Ensemble, Choir, Organ Flutes
7	Bright	Saxophones, Trumpet, Mute Trumpet, Synth Leads, Jazz/Gospel Organs
8	Piano	Piano, Electric Piano, Honky Tonk Piano, Harpsichord, Clavi
9	Novelty	Melodic Percussion, Wah Trumpet, Synth, Whistle, Kazoo, Perc. Organ
10	Bellows	Accordion, French Accordion, Mussette, Harmonica, Pump Organ, Bagpipes

FOR ORGANS, PIANOS & ELECTRONIC KEYBOARDS

E-Z PLAY® TODAY PUBLICATIONS

The E-Z Play® Today songbook series is the shortest distance between beginning music and playing fun!
Check out this list of highlights and visit balleonard.com for a complete listing of all volumes and songlists.

HAL•LEONARD®

Prices, contents and availability subject to change without notice

0421
330